Data Flow Diagrams
Simply Put!

Process Modeling Techniques for
Requirements Elicitation
and Workflow Analysis

Thomas Hathaway
Angela Hathaway

Copyright © 2016 BA-EXPERTS

All rights reserved. No part of this publication may be reproduced, distributed, or transmitted in any form or by any means, including photocopying, recording, or other electronic or mechanical methods, without the prior written permission of the publisher, except in the case of brief quotations embodied in critical reviews and certain other noncommercial uses permitted by copyright law.

The contents of this publication are provided in good faith and neither The Authors nor The Publisher can be held responsible for any errors or omissions contained herein. Any person relying upon the information must independently satisfy himself or herself as to the safety or any other implications of acting upon such information and no liability shall be accepted either by The Authors or The Publisher in the event of reliance upon such information nor for any damage or injury arising from any interpretation of its contents. This publication may not be used in any process of risk assessment.

Ordering Information:

Quantity sales. Special discounts are available on quantity purchases by corporations, associations, and others. For details, contact the publisher at books@BusinessAnalysisExperts.com.

The content of this book is also available as an eCourse at http://businessanalysisexperts.com/product/ecourse-data-flow-diagrams-context-model/

ISBN-10: 1535110139
ISBN-13: 978-1535110136

DEDICATION

This work is dedicated to future generations of Business Analysts, Product Owners, Subject Matter Experts, Domain Experts, COOs, CEOs, Line Managers, and anyone responsible for representing the business community's interests on an Information Technology project.

CONTENTS

DEDICATION i

CONTENTS ii

ACKNOWLEDGMENTS iv

PREFACE v

Introducing Data Flow Diagrams (DFDs) for the Business 7

    Business Processes, Data Flows, and Value Chains 10

    What is a Data Flow Diagram and Why Do You Need One? 13

Modeling the Flow of Material and Data 15

    Introducing Rigorous Physical Process Models to Identify Stakeholders 16

    Drawing an RPPM Using Identified Stakeholders and Interview Notes 20

Visualizing Process Scope 27

How to Identify the "Right" Internal Processes for a DFD 37

    Representing Increasing Levels of Detail Using a DFD 38

    Identifying Candidates for Internal Processes 40

    Selecting the Appropriate Processes to Include on the Detailed DFD 45

Drawing a Detail Level DFD 53

Balancing the Levels Ensures Completeness 67
Balancing Data Flows from the Higher to the Lower Level 69

Balancing Data Flows from the Lower to the Higher Level 74

Creating Detailed Process and Data Specifications 80
Defining Functional Primitives 81

Capturing Metadata for Critical Business Data Elements 88

Horizontal Balancing Reveals Missing Data Elements 93
Defining and Justifying the Value of Horizontal Balancing 94

A Walk-through of Horizontal Balancing 96

The Business Value of Data Flow Diagrams 107
Creating and Using DFD Fragments vs Completely Balanced DFDs 107

Summary 111

What Should You Do Next? 114

ABOUT THE AUTHORS 115

ACKNOWLEDGMENTS

This publication would not have been possible without the active support and hard work of our daughter, Penelope Hathaway. We would also be remiss if we did not acknowledge the thousands of students with whom we have had the honor of working over the years. We can honestly say that every single one of you influenced us in no small way.

Finally, we would like to acknowledge Harvey, the fictional Pooka created by Mary Chase and made famous by the movie of the same name with James Stewart. Very early in our marriage we recognized that a third entity is created and lives whenever we work closely on a concept, a new idea, or a new product. Over the years, this entity became so powerful and important to us that we decided to name it Harvey and he should rightfully be listed as the author of this and all of our creative works. Unfortunately, Harvey remains an invisible being, living somewhere beyond our physical senses but real nonetheless. Without Harvey, neither this book nor any of our other publications would have been possible. For us, Harvey embodies the entity that any collaborative effort creates and he is at least as real as each of us. We would truly be lost without him.

PREFACE

This book was neither created "For Dummies®" nor "For Complete Idiots®", but for normal people in the real world to give them a basic understanding of business analysis concepts and techniques. Many people do business analysis although it is not in their job description.

Whether you are the CEO, COO, Director, Manager, or on the front lines, you may be involved in defining how technology can benefit you and your organization. When you are in that awesome role, you are at that time "the one wearing the Business Analysis (BA) hat".

In today's wired world, software applications often take center stage in optimizing workflow and increasing productivity. Unfortunately, the process of delivering the right software to the right people at the right time is challenging to say the least.

This book presents Data Flow Diagrams (DFDs) as a phenomenal tool for visualizing and analyzing dependencies and interactions amongst manual and automated business processes. It explains what a DFD is, why you need one, and how to create it. You will learn the benefits of process visualization for the business community, for the one wearing the BA hat, for those tasked with developing the solution, and ultimately for the entire organization.

You will also discover how DFDs are powerful tools for recognizing and eliminating two of the major problems that haunt IT projects, namely Scope Creep and Project Overruns caused by late project change requests.

So what are you going to learn? This book presents the nuts and bolts of "requirements elicitation" which will help you:

⇨ Document existing business processes and workflows in Data Flow Diagrams (DFD) to initiate business process analysis

- ⇨ Defend the need for Data Flow Diagrams, Context Diagrams, and Rigorous Physical Process Models

- ⇨ Use the right symbols for each type of diagram to ensure a common interpretation by all parties

- ⇨ Explode a high level Data Flow Diagram to its lower level details to reveal underlying processes and procedures

- ⇨ Balance DFD's to identify missing processes and reduce late project change requests

- ⇨ Use Horizontal Balancing to discover missing data and minimize redundancies

- ⇨ Document process specifications for functional primitives to guide the solution providers

- ⇨ Express metadata to reveal informational details that developers need to build the solution

You can learn more business analysis techniques by visiting the Business Analysis Learning Store at

(http://businessanalysisexperts.com/business-analysis-training-store/)

to see a wide selection of business analysis books, eCourses, virtual and face-to-face instructor-led training, as well as a selection of FREE Business Analysis training.

Meanwhile, please enjoy this book. We appreciate any comments, suggestions, recommended improvements, or complaints that you care to share with us. You can reach us via email at eBooks@businessanalysisexperts.com.

INTRODUCING DATA FLOW DIAGRAMS (DFDS) FOR THE BUSINESS

An old Chinese proverb says, "A picture is worth a thousand words." In the world of Information Technology (IT), we maintain that it may even be worth a whole lot more. For most people, it is difficult or impossible to envision a process flow, especially when someone else is describing it.

In the late 1970's, a concept called "Data Flow Diagramming" became popular as a way to draw a diagram or picture of process interactions and the data created and consumed by each step. This phenomenally simple tool allowed people to visualize their workflow for the first time. Suddenly, disconnects and discrepancies that they had difficulty describing jumped out of the picture at them. It all seems so obvious when you have a simple diagram to analyze.

My partner Angela and I wrote this book to give Business Analysts, System Analysts, Product Owners, Product Managers, Subject Matter Experts (a.k.a. SMEs), and really "anyone wearing the BA hat" a simple, step-by-step approach for creating and using data flow diagrams. Regardless of your job title or role, if you are involved in defining future business solutions with an IT component, this book will empower you to give other people the ability to see how their workflows and business processes or work - and where they need improvement.

In detail, this course explains and demonstrates the answers to these questions:

- ◈ What is a Data Flow Diagram (DFD) and what does it do for you?

- ◈ What is the difference between a Rigorous Physical Process Model and a Context-Level DFD?

- What symbols can you use on each type of diagram?
- What is the business value of exploding or levelling a DFD?
- What is a simple approach for drilling down into a process?
- How can you show the internal processes and flows that produce the results?
- What does balancing a Data Flow Diagram mean and what is the business value?
- What is the most efficient approach to balancing a DFD?
- What business value do detailed process specifications offer?
- How can you express detailed specifications for processes and data?
- What is "metadata" and why do you need it?
- What does a fully balanced DFD look like?
- What value does a DFD fragment provide?
- Why should you draw a Data Flow Diagram?

This book explains what a Data Flow Diagram (DFD) is, why you need one, how to create it, and how to use it to minimize the risk of project failure. Using a business scenario, the course demonstrates how to get started with a Rigorous Physical Process Model (RPPM) based on interview notes, converting the RPPM to a Context DFD, and then exploding the Context DFD to a detailed Data Flow Diagram.

You will learn the benefits of process visualization for the business community, for the one wearing the BA hat, for those tasked with developing the solution, and ultimately for the entire organization.

You will also discover how powerful DFDs are as tools for recognizing and eliminating two of the major problems that haunt IT projects, namely Scope Creep and Project Overruns caused by late project change requests.

Drawing a picture of how a business process creates and consumes data identifies critical functional, informational, and quality (aka non-functional) requirements. Data Flow Diagrams represent that picture.

You will learn why a good DFD is such a phenomenal baseline for identifying problems and defining the business and stakeholder requirements for any IT undertaking.

Business Processes, Data Flows, and Value Chains

A picture really is worth a thousand words, especially in the world of Business Analysis for IT projects. Try to describe workflows or business processes in natural language and the chances that IT will deliver the solution you want are very small indeed. The challenge is what picture do you need to draw?

There are several techniques for drawing process models or diagrams at various levels of detail and each has a specific focus. Data Flow Diagrams (DFDs) represent the workflow or steps within a process with a focus on the flow and transformation of data. You can create DFDs at the business level (as in this example)

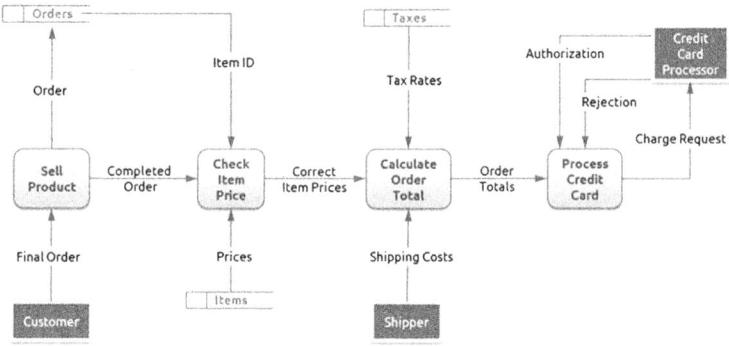

representing business processes and business data or at the system level depicting IT applications, databases, and files. Since we are talking about business analysis, our focus will be creating and using data flow diagrams at the business level.

Every business process is a more-or-less complex sequence of steps that changes something coming in to create something new. As such, the process needs some form of input, which could be information or any other resource. By definition, a data flow diagram is a picture of how the depicted processes create, consume, transport, and store data.

A DFD is the right choice for business process modeling if you need to understand the creation and use of data within the individual business processes. Those processes can be manual or automated; it does not matter as far as the diagram is concerned.

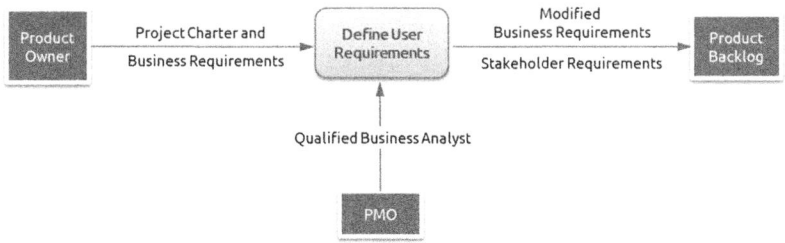

Processes use input to create output, whether the output is something altogether new or simply an altered version of the original input. Since the process adds some measurable value to the input, we often refer to the "value chain" of the organization.

Fundamentally, any diagram is simply a picture with constraints. In the case of the DFD, the constraints are which symbols you can use and what each symbol means. There are really only two widely used conventions for drawing DFDs and the differences are minimal. Both allow only four basic symbols.

A rounded rectangle (or a circle depending on which convention you follow) represents a process at some level of detail. The name of the process tells us what the process does (i.e., what its primary function is) in common business terms. Since functions are actions, the name consists of an active verb (what is done) and a direct object (what is it done to — e.g.,

As you can see from the examples, the named process can be at any level of detail, from the very high-level (*SELL PRODUCT*) to the very low-level (*CHECK ITEM PRICE*).

An arrow represents a data flow, meaning information coming from somewhere and going somewhere else. Because the data is moving from somewhere to somewhere, the arrow points in the direction of movement. Every data flow has to have a name. Because it represents data and data is a thing, the name has to be a noun with or without appropriate modifiers (i.e., *Credit Card Authorization, Invoice, Item Number*). As with the process, the named data flow can be at any level of detail.

CREDIT CARD AUTHORIZATION → **INVOICE** → **ITEM NUMBER** →

A data store is simply data at rest. It is not going anywhere so it cannot be a data flow; it is waiting to be consumed by a process. A data store is not necessarily a file although a file is a data store (like a square is a rectangle but a rectangle is not necessarily a square). A special symbol consisting of a small square with the top and bottom lines extending outward to the right (or simply two parallel lines, again depending on convention) represents a data store.

POLICY HOLDERS

A DFD Makes Scope Visible. A simple square (with or without an optional shadow) represents an external entity. In the world of data flow diagramming, an external entity represents a person, organization, or application that is out of scope for the project from the perspective of the DFD. Specifically, it implies that the represented object is not going to be analyzed or impacted by any project using this diagram although data flows to and from the external entity have to be analyzed.

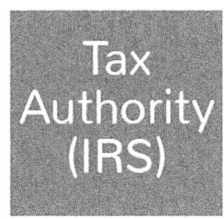

What is a Data Flow Diagram and Why Do You Need One?

A DFD serves multiple purposes. You might create one to be able to analyze the current situation with the goal of identifying roadblocks and improving efficiency. You might also create one to present and discuss the process with others.

You could create a DFD of a proposed business process before you develop detailed processes and supporting IT applications to identify potential issues before they occur. Its principle use is presumably to identify, document, and communicate stakeholder requirements for an IT project.

Fundamentally, there are two good reasons why you need a diagram. First off, people can point to the diagram to discuss a process or flow instead of using words to describe what they mean. The diagram represents a visual mode of communication, which all studies show is much more effective than mere words. Pointing power proves that it works.

Secondly, studying the diagram generates questions that might indicate missing steps or external entities. If the diagram piques your curiosity, it is well worth your while to investigate the situation to find an answer.

Online resources for you:

Watch this chapter in video format

- ⇨ Business Processes, Data Flows, and Value Chains
  https://www.youtube.com/watch?v=0izbsoxHipg

- ⇨ What is a Data Flow Diagram and Why Do You Need One?
  https://www.youtube.com/watch?v=kBeUY8noj6A

More resources

- ⇨ FREE video: Business Process Analysis for Requirements Discovery
  http://businessanalysisexperts.com/product/business-process-analysis-requirements-definition/

- ⇨ An Introduction to Data Flow Diagrams
  http://www.modernanalyst.com/Resources/Articles/tabid/115/ID/2009/An-Introduction-to-Data-Flow-Diagrams.aspx

- ⇨ Introduction to Data Flow Diagrams
  https://www.cs.uct.ac.za/mit_notes/SE/Jul2009/html/ch03s02.html

MODELING THE FLOW OF MATERIAL AND DATA

Questions answered in this chapter:

- What is a Rigorous Physical Process Model (RPPM) and why do I need one?
- What symbols does it use?
- How can I create an RPPM from interview notes?

Once you have taken the first step, namely deciding that drawing a Data Flow Diagram would benefit your project, the next question is typically, "OK, where do I start?" There are many potential answers to that question.

In this chapter, we introduce a concept called a "Rigorous Physical Process Model" as one of the simplest ways of getting started that we know. You will learn why this simple tool is extremely useful as a starting point for the DFD and how to create your own Rigorous Physical Process Models.

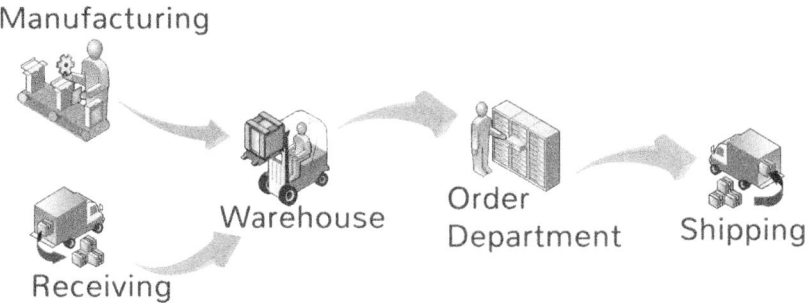

Introducing Rigorous Physical Process Models to Identify Stakeholders

A Rigorous Physical Process Model shows the movement of physical objects and data amongst the units in an organization. The idea is to represent the real world as closely as possible. Given that the proposed information technology (IT) solution will need to know something about the physical objects, these will have to be represented in data as well.

The power of an RPPM lies in its simplicity. It only allows two symbols, a circle to represent people or places and an arrow representing the movement of physical material or data. This simplicity makes it easy to implement and it is an ideal precursor to a Data Flow Diagram.

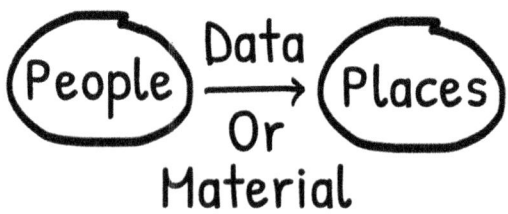

Creating a Rigorous Physical Process Model is a step by step process based on the analysis of any information you have available (e.g. interview results, procedure manuals, help- facilities, etc.).

Now that you know the symbols for creating an RPPM, I would like to walk you through the exercise of analyzing a situation to create one using a standard scenario from our instructor-led class.

FYI, on the next page you will find a transcript of an interview with the Manager of the Order Entry Department, Mary (the project sponsor).

Interview Notes

The customer triggers all the action in our department. We receive an order (with or without payment), a complaint or a payment (with or without invoice copy) from the customer. These are separated and the following actions take place:

If it is an order, we verify an existing customer's credit status and then we verify that the item numbers are valid by checking our inventory file. New customer's orders are sent to the credit department and held until they clear a credit check. (If half payment or more is included, that order is treated as if it were a credit order with good credit.)

Valid orders are accumulated and grouped into shipping zones and transmitted to the warehouse to be filled. After an order is filled, the customer address is attached, the best or requested shipping method determined, postage or shipping costs calculated, the order is shipped, and the warehouse inventory is reduced. A copy of the packing slip goes to accounting where an invoice is created and sent to the customer, and the customer's account updated. Copies of orders with payments and payments go to accounting, where the payments are applied to the customer's account. The item inventory is officially updated in accounting.

Customer complaints go directly to customer service. They research the situation and respond to the customer as soon as possible. Any action taken by customer service, which affects accounting or inventory, is passed to them for updating. Possible actions are a new order, a debit, or a credit. These look exactly like the regular order process.

My approach is to read the text and look for people and places that I want to represent in my RPPM. When I find a noun, I decide whether it names a person or place on my process model or simply names data or physical material I need to track. I'll try my best, but don't have to be perfect as this is my first cut at it.

Interview Notes

The **customer** triggers all the action in **our department**. We receive an order (with or without payment), a complaint or a payment (with or without invoice copy) from the customer. These are separated and the following actions take place:

If it is an order, we verify an existing customer's credit status and then we verify that the item numbers are valid by checking our inventory file. New customer's orders are sent to the **credit department** and held until they clear a credit check. (If half payment or more is included, that order is treated as if it were a credit order with good credit.)

Valid orders are accumulated and grouped into shipping zones and transmitted to the warehouse to be filled. After an order is filled, the customer address is attached, the best or requested shipping method determined, postage or shipping costs calculated, the order is shipped, and the **warehouse** inventory is reduced. A copy of the packing slip goes to accounting where an invoice is created and sent to the customer, and the customer's account updated. Copies of orders with payments and payments go to **accounting**, where the payments are applied to the customer's account. The item inventory is officially updated in accounting.

> Customer complaints go directly to **customer service**. They research the situation and respond to the customer as soon as possible. Any action taken by customer service, which affects accounting or inventory, is passed to them for updating. Possible actions are a new order, a debit, or a credit. These look exactly like the regular order process.

I usually use color-coding or underlining while I am doing this. I underlined five nouns that I think represent people or places (CUSTOMER, our department – aka ORDER ENTRY, CREDIT DEPARTMENT, WAREHOUSE, ACCOUNTING, and CUSTOMER SERVICE).

There are a lot of other nouns in the narrative, but I think they are all simply things I may need to keep track of, so I am going to ignore them for now. At this time, I am only interested in people and places (in this case, organizational units) where the data might come from or go to.

Drawing an RPPM Using Identified Stakeholders and Interview Notes

Since the text indicates that everything starts with the customer, I start my diagram by drawing a circle in the upper left-hand corner of the page and labeling it CUSTOMER.

The next part mentioned in the narrative is 'our department', so I draw another circle diagonally to the right of and below the CUSTOMER and name it ORDER ENTRY. Since I will add flows between the entities, I need to leave room enough for a label and one or more arrows between the two circles.

Analyzing the narrative, I see that ORDER ENTRY receives *Orders, Payments, and Complaints* from the CUSTOMER, so I draw the arrow indicating the flow from the CUSTOMER to ORDER ENTRY and label it respectively.

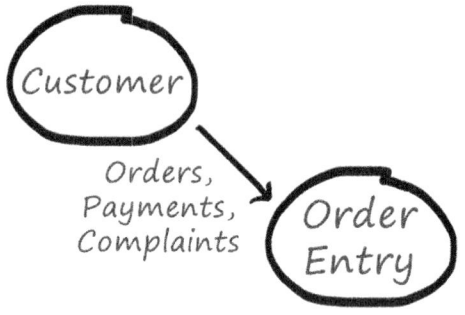

Next, I read several things that ORDER ENTRY does with the incoming flow. I am going to be interested in these specific actions later (once I know the scope of this project) but for the time being, I am ignoring them. All I am really interested in at this time is the flow of data between departments and not what each department does with it.

Because of that, the next flow I find in the narrative is that ORDER ENTRY sends new customer orders to the CREDIT DEPARTMENT. That causes me to add a circle diagonally above and to the right of the ORDER ENTRY symbol, labelling it CREDIT

DEPARTMENT, adding an arrow from ORDER ENTRY to the CREDIT DEPARTMENT, and labelling the arrow *New Customer Order*. Again, I need to make sure the spacing between the circles leaves room for the arrow and its label.

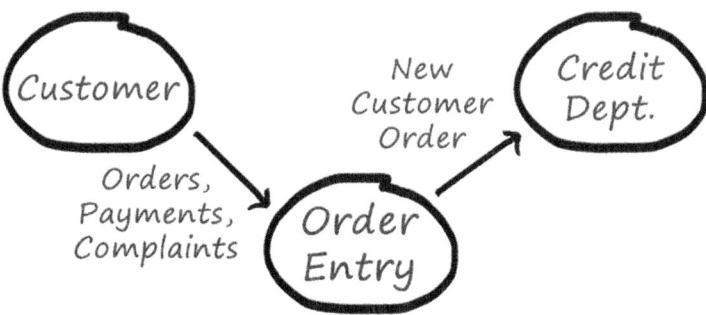

Reading on, I note that *valid orders* are transmitted to the WAREHOUSE, so I add a circle labelled "WAREHOUSE" below the one labelled CREDIT DEPARTMENT and add a *Valid Order* arrow originating from ORDER ENTRY.

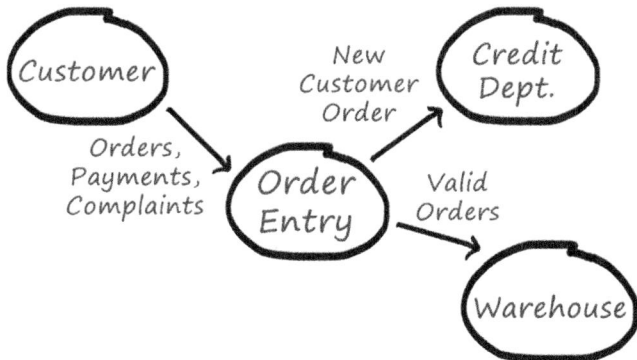

As you can by now surmise, I am trying to draw the diagram diagonally from the upper left to the lower right of the page following the flow of the order as expressed in the narrative. The major reason for this is cultural. English and many other languages are written from left to right starting at the top of the page and continue down to the bottom. If my diagram conforms to this convention, it is easier for most people to follow.

Back to the narrative, the next flow of data that I note is the WAREHOUSE shipping the order to the customer. To represent this flow, I could draw an arrow from the WAREHOUSE around the CREDIT DEPARTMENT back to the CUSTOMER but that would violate my left-to-right, top-to-bottom flow. Since I consider the readability of the diagram to be critical, I'm going to 'cheat' by adding a second circle labelled CUSTOMER /2 (indicating that this symbol is a repeat) diagonally below and to the right of the WAREHOUSE symbol and insert an arrow labelled *Shipment* from the WAREHOUSE to the CUSTOMER /2 symbol. This positioning keeps the directional flow intact.

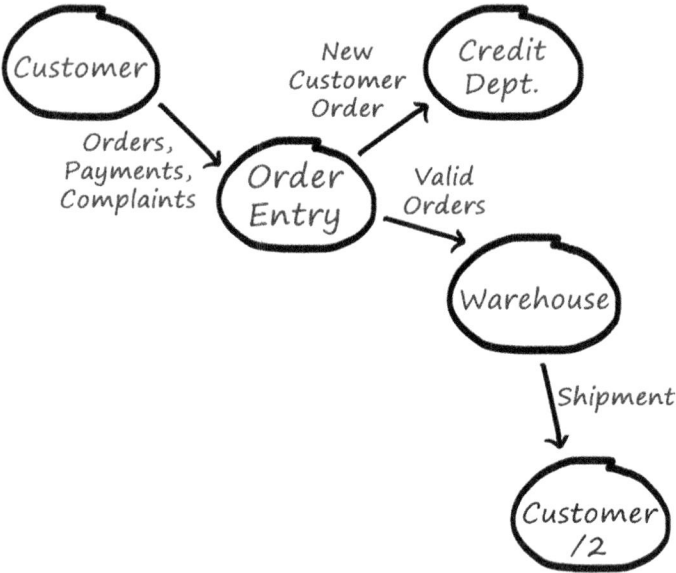

Next, I read a copy of the Packing Slip goes from the WAREHOUSE to ACCOUNTING, so I add an appropriately labelled circle below, to the left of the WAREHOUSE symbol, and add the flow *Copy of Packing Slip* from the WAREHOUSE to ACCOUNTING.

ACCOUNTING sends an invoice to the customer which I represent with an arrow labelled *invoice* from ACCOUNTING to CUSTOMER /2, again maintaining the proper reading direction of the diagram.

When I read 'copies of orders with payments and payments go to accounting', I have to backtrack to the beginning of the narrative to discover that these are coming from the CUSTOMER to ORDER ENTRY, so this simply adds a new flow from ORDER ENTRY to ACCOUNTING with the label *Copy of Order with Payment, Payments.*

Updating the Item Inventory is internal to ACCOUNTING, so it does not concern me here.

The final paragraph is a bit more confusing. First off, complaints go directly to CUSTOMER SERVICE. Again, by rereading the first paragraph, I recognize that ORDER ENTRY received the complaints, so I add the arrow *complaints* going from ORDER ENTRY to CUSTOMER SERVICE.

CUSTOMER SERVICE sends a *Response* to the customer which is an arrow between CUSTOMER SERVICE and CUSTOMER /2.

In reading the actions CUSTOMER SERVICE takes, I conclude that I also need a flow labeled *Debit or Credit* from CUSTOMER SERVICE to ACCOUNTING and a *New Order* flow from CUSTOMER SERVICE back to the ORDER ENTRY department (which makes these "look exactly like the regular order process" as expressed in the interview notes).

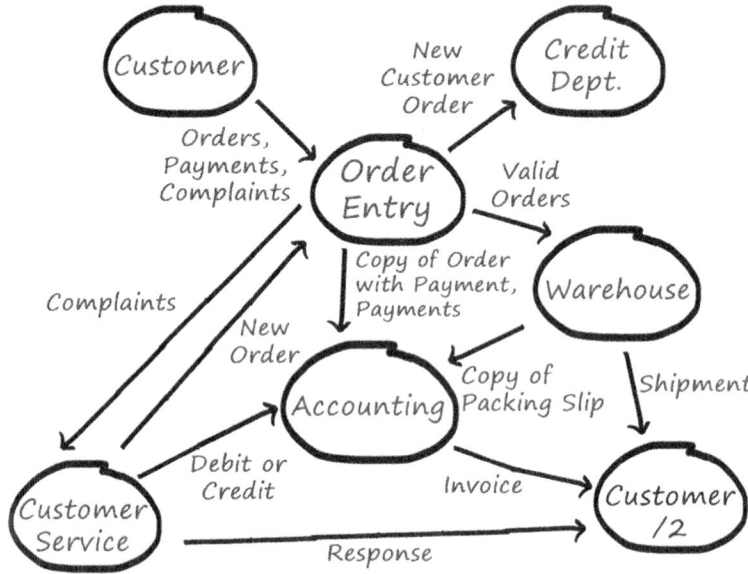

I now have a picture of the process (aka. Rigorous Physical Process Model) depicted in the interview notes from Mary. I can use it to present the process to any audience. We can focus our discussions about the process by pointing at the various units and flows.

A simple, clear picture like this increases comprehension and retention. Once I have gained Mary's approval that my diagram is an accurate representation of the process flow, we can initiate the process of morphing this Rigorous Physical Process Model into a legitimate Data Flow Diagram.

Online resources for you:

Watch part of this chapter as a FREE video

⇨ Create a Rigorous Physical Process Model as an Easy Start to a Data Flow Diagram
https://www.youtube.com/watch?v=KzAbxnpDGpo

More resources

⇨ Data Flow Diagram (DFD)
http://myyee.tripod.com/cs457/dfd.htm

⇨ Hottest 'dataflow-diagram' Answers - Stack Overflow
http://stackoverflow.com/tags/dataflow-diagram/hot

⇨ FREE Business Analysis Training
http://businessanalysisexperts.com/product-category/free-business-analysis-training/

VISUALIZING PROCESS SCOPE

Questions answered in this chapter:

- What is the difference between a Rigorous Physical Process Model and a Context-Level DFD?
- How can I convert the RPPM to a legitimate DFD?
- Why is this conversion necessary??

At the very beginning of any project, one of the most important decisions that someone has to make is, "What are the boundaries of this project?" or, put differently, "What is the project scope?" With only the authority of the one wearing the BA hat, I cannot make a decision regarding the scope of the project. A project sponsor (the common title for the individual in the organization who is funding the project) or someone with similar authority has to define the project scope.

Because "scope creep" is a significant risk on IT projects, we not only need someone with the proper authority to define the scope, we have to represent their decision in a form that everyone involved with the project can visualize, understand, and defend.

One of the simplest tools for visualizing project scope is a Context-level Data Flow Diagram (DFD). Beyond making the project scope visible, a DFD will ultimately allow us to discover, analyze, and represent functional and non-functional requirements.

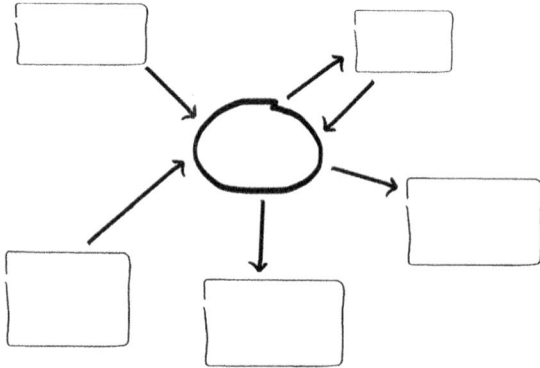

This chapter will give you a very easy-to-follow transition from a Rigorous Physical Process Model depicting the flow of physical goods and information into a Context-Level Data Flow Diagram (aka "Level 1" or sometimes "Level 0") that is a picture of the scope of your IT project.

Once you have the picture, use it to vigorously defend the scope boundaries and, if they change, update the model. It is quick, simple, and gives you an extremely powerful visual tool for presenting and defending the scope of your project. Use it as a weapon to defeat the dreaded "Scope Creep" monster that plagues so many IT projects.

Convert an RPPM to a Context DFD

At the end of the last chapter, we created a diagram of the situation described in the narrative (interview notes).

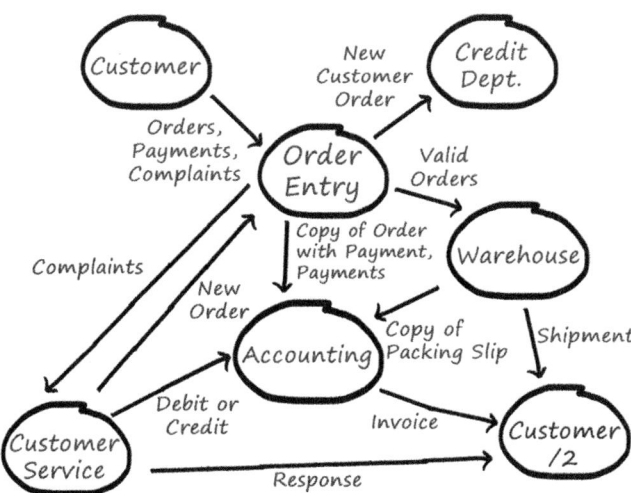

The problem is that it does not follow the rules governing symbols on a Data Flow Diagram. All I have are circles with NOUN names but according to the rules, circles represent *PROCESSES* on a DFD and *PROCESSES* have to have a *VERB/OBJECT* name (do something to something)!

The reason for this is that I drew the Rigorous Physical Process Model without knowing which of these depicted people and places are in scope for my project and which are not. I need to get an answer to the scope question to convert this Rigorous Physical Process Model to a Context Data Flow Diagram.

As the one wearing the BA hat, I cannot make a decision regarding the scope of the project. That decision ultimately has to be made by the project sponsor (the common title for the individual in the organization who is funding the project). Mary is our project sponsor and the Department Manager of Order Entry. Her authority is limited to anything the Order Entry Department does. Based on her authority, I can now convert my initial diagram by following a few simple rules.

First off, since ORDER ENTRY is in scope for my project, I need to change the noun ORDER ENTRY to a VERB/OBJECT to make it a legitimate function. What I look for is the primary function that ORDER ENTRY performs and Mary agrees that their primary function is to *ENTER ORDERS*.

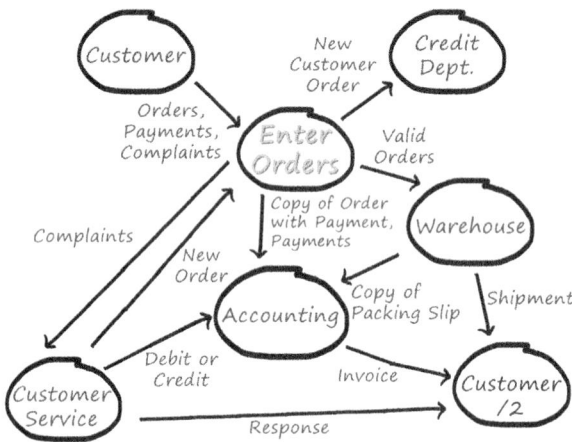

By changing the name of the circle from the department ORDER ENTRY to the function *ENTER ORDERS*, I not only have a legitimate function, I also made a critical psychological shift. As the project progresses, I am going to analyze what happens inside the *ENTER ORDERS* process which will lead to the recognition that there are several problems with how the unit currently processes orders (that's why the project was initiated).

If I leave the name of the object ORDER ENTRY, I would be accusing the department of making errors, which leads to pointing fingers and making accusations. This can result in a lot of pushback from the employees in the department as they feel unjustly criticized.

Having changed the name from the department to the function, I can critically analyze the *ENTER ORDERS* function and find flaws in it. In this case, the same employees will join in enthusiastically because the problems are caused by the process and it is not their fault. This seemingly simple step can literally make or break the project.

Next, I convert all other circles on the diagram to squares to turn them into legitimate external entities to get to an almost legitimate DFD.

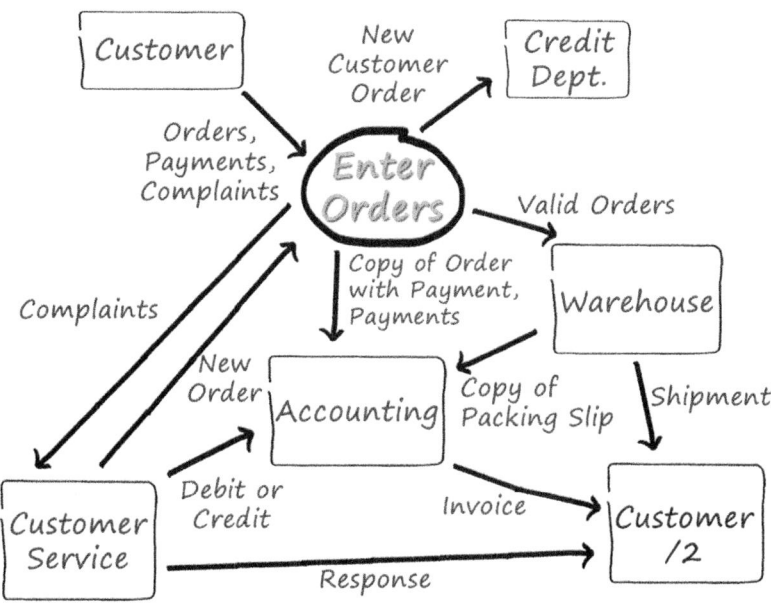

The only remaining problem is that the diagram violates a simple but powerful rule of data flow diagramming, namely that flows between two external entities are logically out of scope (since both ends of the flow are out of scope).

To comply with that rule, I eliminate the Debit or Credit flow from CUSTOMER SERVICE to ACCOUNTING and the flow Response from CUSTOMER SERVICE to CUSTOMER /2. I can further ignore the Shipment flow from the WAREHOUSE to CUSTOMER /2, the Copy of Packing Slip from the WAREHOUSE to

ACCOUNTING, and the Invoice flow from ACCOUNTING to CUSTOMER /2.

After eliminating all of these out-of-scope flows, I see that the CUSTOMER /2 entity I had added to maintain the logical left-to-right, top-down flow is unnecessary since it is no longer involved in any data flows, so I can also delete it.

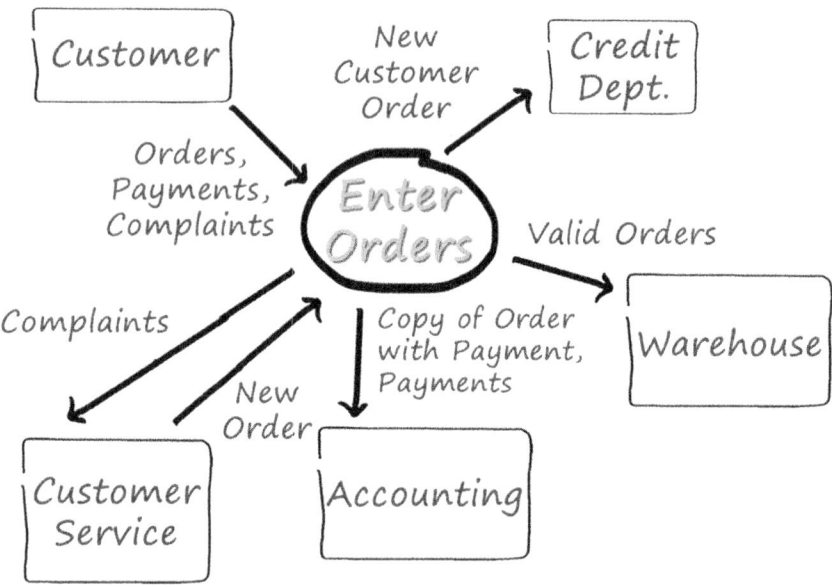

I now have a perfectly legitimate Context Level Data Flow Diagram (aka a "Context Diagram", a "Level 0 [Zero] DFD", or sometimes a "Level 1 DFD") for the project. Note that every flow on the diagram either goes into or comes out of the one process on the diagram that is in scope, namely *ENTER ORDERS*. That is one of the hallmarks of a good Context Level DFD. Its primary reason for being is to manage the scope of the project.

Assuming my diagram is an accurate representation of the situation, anything done during the *ENTER ORDERS* process is in scope and subject to change; everything else is out of scope for this project.

Data Flow Diagrams - *Simply Put!*

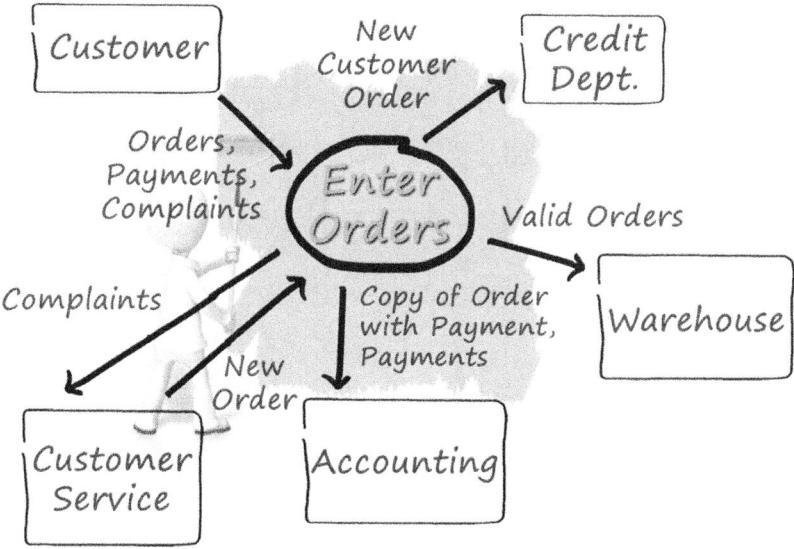

If anyone starts to discuss problems with selecting the best shipping method for a shipment (based on the narrative this is done in the WAREHOUSE), I point to the diagram to show why that problem is irrelevant to the current scope of the project and therefore we should not spend project resources discussing it.

When I look at this diagram, I recognize a different problem. I am sending New Customer Orders to the CREDIT DEPARTMENT where according to the narrative they are 'held until they clear a credit check'. That begs the question, 'What happens to them once they have cleared the credit check?' What does the CREDIT DEPARTMENT do with them?

When I pose that question to my project sponsor, she explains that the CREDIT DEPARTMENT sends approved orders back to ORDER ENTRY, which ODER ENTRY has to continue processing the same as other orders from known customers with good credit. That fact causes me to add the flow Credit OK Orders from the CREDIT DEPARTMENT to the *ENTER ORDERS* process.

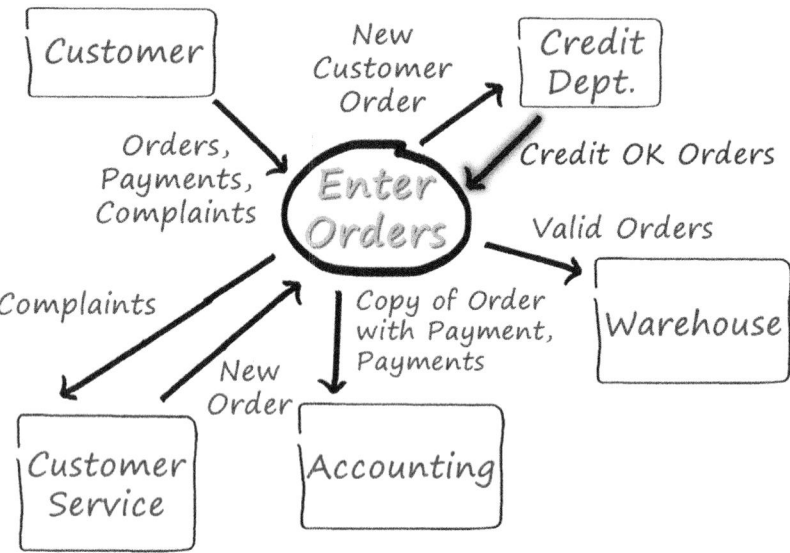

As a side note, it is not unusual to discover missing flows such as this once you start to work with the Context Level DFD. The earlier in the project that you can identify them, the cheaper it is to incorporate them into your project work. By the way, if you identified this issue while you were creating the original diagram and added this flow at that time, kudos, you are one step ahead of me.

Online resources for you:

- ⇨ Context diagrams
  https://www.cs.uct.ac.za/mit_notes/SE/Jul2009/html/ch03s07.html

- ⇨ Data Flow Diagram (DFD) Tutorial
  https://www.visual-paradigm.com/tutorials/data-flow-diagram-dfd.jsp

- ⇨ Example of a DFD Context Diagram
  https://www.youtube.com/watch?v=zQvmrmvqyS4

- ⇨ Context Diagrams
  http://kinzz.com/resources/articles/110-context-diagram?showall=1

- ⇨ Data Flow Diagram Tutorial – Rohan
  http://www-rohan.sdsu.edu/~haytham/dfd_tutorial.htm

- ⇨ *Context Level, Level 0 & Level 1 DFDs*
  https://prezi.com/dcsxbohjlihe/context-level-level-0-level-1-dfds/

HOW TO IDENTIFY THE "RIGHT" INTERNAL PROCESSES FOR A DFD

Questions answered in this chapter:

- What does "exploding a process" mean?
- What is the business value of doing it?
- What processes will the lower level diagram contain?

As useful as a Context-Level (DFD) is, it is sorely lacking in detail. In this chapter, we present a straight-forward approach for "exploding" or "levelling" a DFD to depict processes and data at increasing levels of detail.

Once you have a list of potential processes that you might want to include on your lower level diagram, you have to figure out which to use to avoid overloading the diagram. We present a technique for identifying potential processes to include at each level and explain how to pick the best candidates for your situation.

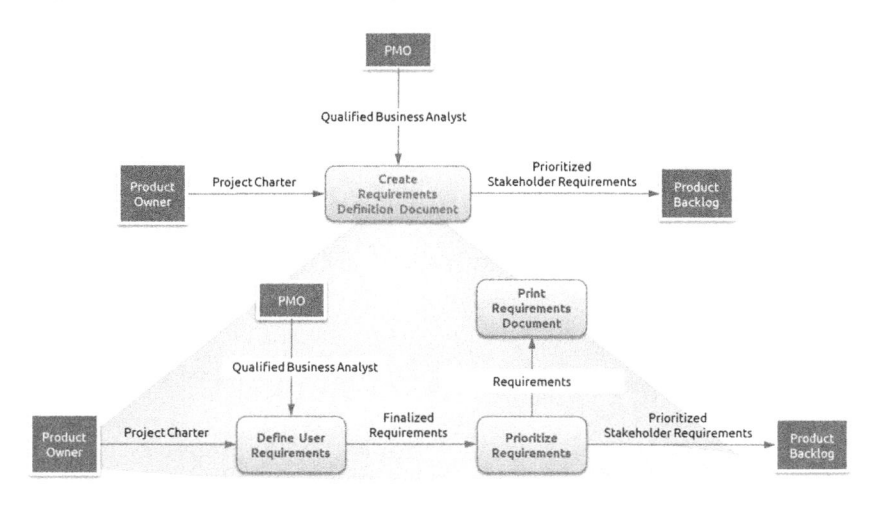

Representing Increasing Levels of Detail Using a DFD

As revealing and useful as a Context Diagram may be, it is certainly lacking a lot of detail. In Data Flow Diagramming lingo, the detail is revealed by "exploding" or "levelling" complex processes (e.g. *ENTER ORDERS*) to identify internal processes and flows that are not visible at the higher level.

By exploding a process, you will also identify internal data stores, meaning places where the data just sits within the process waiting until it is used by another process. Delving into this level of detail may allow you to discover additional missing flows such as the *Credit OK Orders* flow we dealt with previously.

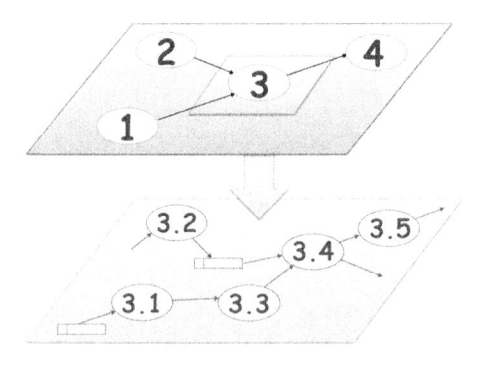

Each of these internal processes creates and consumes specific data. If you draw a data flow diagram at this more detailed level, you uncover internal data flows and data stores that are more specific and detailed as well.

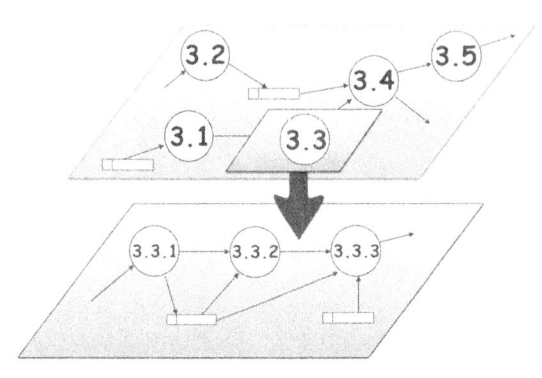

Any process at any level of detail is a potential candidate for exploding. The only factor to consider is whether you understand the process sufficiently to predict how change will affect it.

For example, to analyze how the *ENTER ORDERS* process works, I need details. To represent it, I am going to look inside the *ENTER ORDERS* process and define how it currently works.

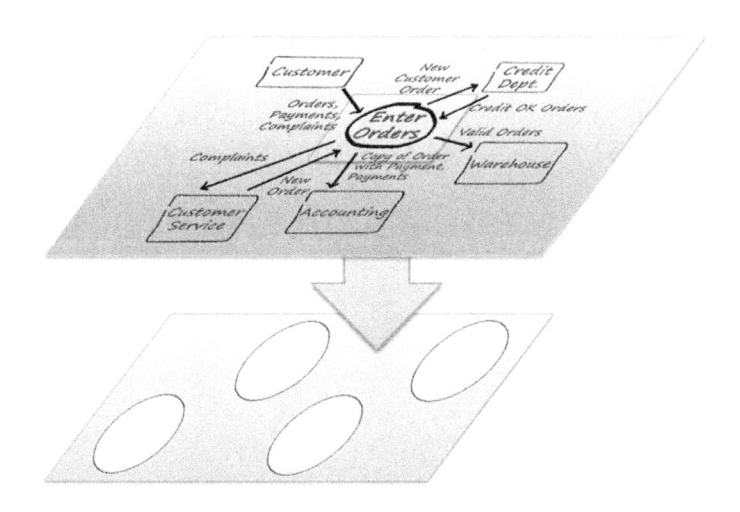

Identifying Candidates for Internal Processes

Before you can explode a high-level process, you need to identify the detailed processes that you could use on a lower level Data Flow Diagram. Selecting the right processes for the lower level can be a daunting task due to the overwhelming number of possibilities. In the remainder of this chapter, I will demonstrate how to select appropriate processes for the lower level diagram.

Given that all I have at this time are my interview notes from the project sponsor, I start by analyzing them to find these lower-level details.

Interview Notes

The customer triggers all the action in our department. We receive an order (with or without payment), a complaint, or a payment (with or without invoice copy) from the customer. These are separated and the following actions take place:

If it is an order, we *(obscured)* n ex *(obscured)* g cust *(obscured)* s *(obscured)* edit status and then we verify that the item numbers are valid by checking our i *(obscured)* omer *(obscured)* rs sent to *(obscured)* ed *(obscured)* p *(obscured)* d *(obscured)* hey clear a credit check. *(obscured)* e is *(obscured)* t *(obscured)* rder is t *(obscured)* if it w *(obscured)* cre *(obscured)* ith good credit.)

Valid orde *(obscured)* e ac *(obscured)* ed *(obscured)* into *(obscured)* and t *(obscured)* mitt *(obscured)* d *(obscured)* filled. After an order is filled, the c *(obscured)* omer address is atta *(obscured)* ed. The *(obscured)* ted shipping method determined, postage or shipping costs calculated, *(obscured)* order is ship *(obscured)* and the waren *(obscured)* is reduced. A copy of the packing slip goes to accounting where an invoice is created and sent to the custo *(obscured)* tomer's account updated. Copies of orders with payments and payments go to accounting, where the payments *(obscured)* to the customer's account. The item inventory is officially updated in accounting.

Customer complaints go directly to customer service. They research the situation and respond to the customer as soon as possible. Any action taken by customer service, which affects accounting or inventory, is passed to them for updating. Possible actions are a new order, a debit, or a credit. These look exactly like the regular order process.

Specifically, I am looking for actions that represent lower level processes performed within *ENTER ORDERS*.

RULE 1 — I will only accept verbs in their active voice (e.g., 'enter orders' is active whereas 'orders are entered' is passive). When I find a verb in the passive voice, I convert it to active voice to evaluate if it is a legitimate process. I give each prospect a proper active-verb-direct-object name as recommended for naming processes on a DFD (e.g., Check Inventory, Separate Mail).

... orders are entered ... ⇨ Enter Orders

⬇ ⬇

ACTIVE VERB   **DIRECT OBJECT**

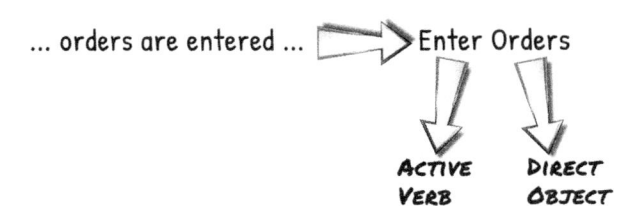

To make sure that my lower level diagram is an accurate depiction of how the *ENTER ORDERS* process really works today, I involve a representative from the group who actually does the work. Managers typically do not need to know the level of detail that I need. Assuming they were promoted from the ranks, they probably know how they did the work back then but they may not be up to date on exactly how the work is done today.

To get a truly accurate and current picture of the *ENTER ORDERS* process, I review the narrative and identify the internal processes with Paul, an Order Entry Clerk.

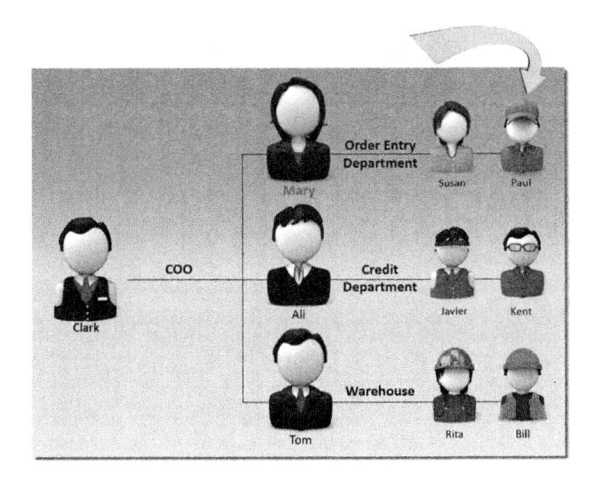

Since processes on a DFD are actions, we simply look for verbs stating or implying actions and create a simple table.

Let me demonstrate this process.

41

The first thing we find in the notes from Mary, Manager of Order Entry Department,

> # Interview Notes
>
> The customer triggers all the action in our department. We receive an order (with or without payment), a complaint or a payment (with or without invoice copy) from the customer. These are separated and the following actions take place:
>
> If it is an order, we verify an existing customer's credit status and then we verify that the item numbers are valid by checking our inventory file. New customer's orders are sent to the credit department and held until they clear a credit check. (If half payment or more is included, that order is treated as if it were a credit order with good credit.)
>
> Valid orders are accumulated and grouped into shipping zones and transmitted to the warehouse to be filled. After an order is filled, the customer address is attached, the best or requested shipping method determined, postage or shipping costs calculated, the order is shipped, and the warehouse inventory is reduced. A copy of the packing slip goes to accounting where an invoice is created and sent to the customer, and the customer's account updated. Copies of orders with payments and payments go to accounting, where the payments are applied to the customer's account. The item inventory is officially updated in accounting.
>
> Customer complaints go directly to customer service. They research the situation and respond to the customer as soon as possible. Any action taken by customer service, which affects accounting or inventory, is passed to them for updating. Possible actions are a new order, a debit, or a credit. These look exactly like the regular order process.

"*The customer triggers all the action in our department.*" TRIGGER ACTION is an active verb with a direct object so I jot it down as a likely candidate. Reading on,

"*We receive an order (with or without payment), a complaint, or a payment (with or without invoice copy) from the customer.*" Receive is certainly an action, so I add "RECEIVE ORDERS, COMPLAINTS, AND PAYMENTS" to my list of potential processes.

"*These are separated and the following actions take place.*" "Are separated' is the passive form of the active verb "'to separate'", but the action SEPARATE THESE does not make any sense. What are they separating? I suggest, "Separate Orders, Complaints, and Payments" but that just repeats what they received and Paul explains they call it SORT MAIL. That is short and says it all, so I add that to my list.

"*If it is an order, we verify an existing customer's credit status*" ... I can certainly see VERIFY CREDIT as a candidate.

"*... and then we verify that the item numbers are valid ...*" To distinguish this action from the VERIFY CREDIT action I just added, I prefer to call this VALIDATE ITEMS and Paul has no objection.

"*... by checking our inventory file. New customer's orders are sent to the credit department ...*" Aha, "Send Orders to Credit" makes my list and for simplicity Paul suggests shortening that to SEND ORDERS.

"*... and held until they clear a credit check.*" HOLD ORDERS is a legitimate candidate and makes the list.

"*(If half payment or more is included, that order is treated as if it were a credit order with good credit.)*" I am not too sure what to do with this parenthetical phrase right now, so I make a note to revisit this later.

"*Valid orders are accumulated ...*" I think ACCUMULATE VALID ORDERS has potential as an internal process.

"*... and grouped into shipping zones ...*" GROUP ORDERS makes the list.

"*... and transmitted to the warehouse to be filled.*" TRANSMIT VALID ORDERS sounds good to me so I add it.

"*After an order is filled ...*" FILL ORDER is an active verb with a direct object, so it makes the list as well.

Interview Notes

The customer <u>triggers all the action</u> in our department. We <u>receive an order</u> (with or without payment), <u>a complaint or a payment</u> (with or without invoice copy) from the customer. <u>These are separated</u> and the following actions take place:

If it is an order, we <u>verify an existing customer's credit status</u> and then we <u>verify that the item numbers are valid</u> by checking our inventory file. <u>New customer's orders are sent to the credit department</u> and held until they clear a credit check. (If half payment or more is included, that order is treated as if it were a credit order with good credit.)

<u>Valid orders are accumulated</u> and <u>grouped into shipping zones</u> and <u>transmitted to the warehouse</u> to be filled. After an <u>order is filled</u>, ...

I could continue reading through the entire interview notes, but I think this suffices to give you the flavor of the process. For practice, you might want to review the remaining interview notes and complete this step on your own.

Selecting the Appropriate Processes to Include on the Detailed DFD

This technique can lead to an overwhelming number of candidate processes for a lower level DFD. Ideally, the ensuing diagram should contain 5-9 processes. Here, I present 2 additional simple rules designed to ferret out the "right" processes for inclusion at the next level of detail.

I will use the list of potential internal processes that we identified and apply the following two new rules to confirm that our identified processes are indeed good candidates.

Candidates (excerpts from interview notes)	**Rule 1:** Verb-Object
The customer **triggers** all action ...	TRIGGER ACTION
... **receive** orders, complaints, and payments...	RECEIVE ORDERS, COMPLAINTS, PMNTS
These **are separated** ...	SORT MAIL
... **verify** an existing customer's credit status ...	VERIFY CREDIT
... **verify** that the item numbers are valid ...	VALIDATE ITEMS
New customer's orders **are sent** to the credit department ...	SEND ORDERS
... **held** until they clear a credit check ...	HOLD ORDERS
... Valid orders **are accumulated** ...	ACCUMULATE ORDERS
... and **grouped** into shipping zones ...	GROUP ORDERS
... **transmitted** to the Warehouse to be filled ...	TRANSMIT VALID ORDERS
An order **is filled** ...	FILL ORDER
...	...

RULE 2 Processes have to do something that will ultimately be represented in the form of data. In other words, a process **transforms incoming data into outgoing data**. If the action affects physical material (e.g., '*Shipment*'), the application will have to know something about the material.

```
Brainstormed  →  Define User  →  Finalized      →  Prioritize
Requirements     Requirements    Requirements      Requirements
```

RULE 3 Secondly, what the process does has to be **within the scope of the process** I am analyzing (in this case, *ENTER ORDERS*).

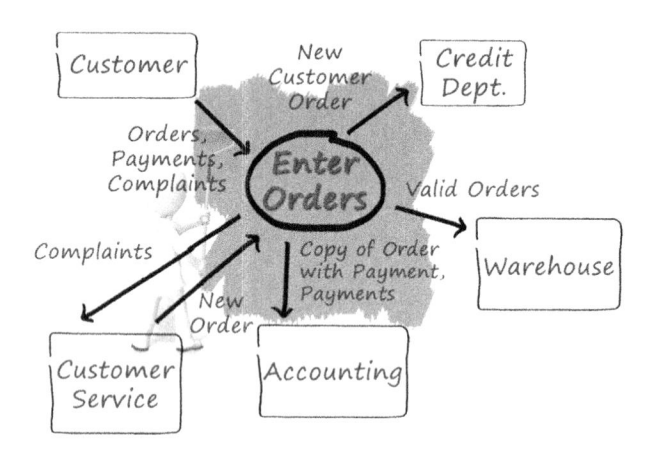

```
Customer → Orders, Payments, Complaints → Enter Orders
New Customer Order → Credit Dept.
Enter Orders → Valid Orders → Warehouse
Enter Orders → Copy of Order with Payment, Payments → Accounting
Enter Orders → New Order → Customer Service
Customer Service → Complaints → (back)
```

Each action on my list that meets these 2 rules is an internal process that should show up on my lower level diagram of the process *ENTER ORDERS*. All I have to do is go through each row in my table and ask a couple of easy-to-answer questions.

Starting with *TRIGGER ACTION*, I ask Paul if that action creates any new data. He confirms that it does not. Our discussion reveals that *TRIGGER ACTION* is not something the ORDER ENTRY personnel do meaning it is Out of Scope. As a result, I jot down "No" in the column indicating whether this will show up on the exploded diagram.

Rule 1: Verb-Object?	**Rule 2:** Transforms Data?	**Rule 3:** In Scope?	**Internal Process** Yes/No
TRIGGER ACTION	NO	OUT	NO

Moving on, Paul explains that *RECEIVE DOCUMENTS* is just someone picking up the mail which also does not create any new data. As a result, it is also Not an Internal Process.

Rule 1: Verb-Object?	**Rule 2:** Transforms Data?	**Rule 3:** In Scope?	**Internal Process** Yes/No
RECEIVE ORDER, COMPLAINTS, PAYMENTS	NO	IN	NO

SORT MAIL on the other hand actually changes things by separating Orders, Complaints, and Payments into three separate stacks for further processing. Since this is done by the Order Entry Clerk assigned that duty for the day, it is a legitimate internal process.

Rule 1: Verb-Object?	**Rule 2:** Transforms Data?	**Rule 3:** In Scope?	**Internal Process** Yes/No
SORT MAIL	YES	IN	YES

VERIFY CREDIT results in the clerk stamping the order "Credit OK", "Credit Not OK", or "New Customer". Those actions create new data which makes *VERIFY CREDIT* an internal process of interest.

Rule 1: Verb-Object?	**Rule 2:** Transforms Data?	**Rule 3:** In Scope?	**Internal Process** Yes/No
VERIFY CREDIT	YES	IN	YES

VALIDATE ITEMS separates orders on which all item numbers and descriptions match items in our Inventory File from orders with mismatches which also makes it a good internal process.

Rule 1: Verb-Object?	**Rule 2:** Transforms Data?	**Rule 3:** In Scope?	**Internal Process** Yes/No
VALIDATE ITEMS	YES	IN	YES

SEND ORDERS to the Credit Department does not add any data so it is not an internal process of interest.

Rule 1: Verb-Object?	**Rule 2:** Transforms Data?	**Rule 3:** In Scope?	**Internal Process** Yes/No
SEND ORDERS	NO	IN	NO

HOLD ORDERS is actually something the Credit Department does which makes it out of scope for the ENTER ORDERS process, again eliminating it as an internal process for our purposes.

Rule 1: Verb-Object?	Rule 2: Transforms Data?	Rule 3: In Scope?	Internal Process Yes/No
HOLD ORDERS	NO	OUT	NO

ACCUMULATE VALID ORDERS does not add new data since it is simply adding valid orders to a stack until it is time to send them to the warehouse.

Rule 1: Verb-Object?	Rule 2: Transforms Data?	Rule 3: In Scope?	Internal Process Yes/No
ACCUMULATE VALID ORDERS	NO	IN	NO

To prepare the valid orders for the WAREHOUSE, the Order Entry clerk has to GROUP ORDERS into shipping zones which does add new data (the shipping zone) to each order meaning this is another valid internal process.

Rule 1: Verb-Object?	Rule 2: Transforms Data?	Rule 3: In Scope?	Internal Process Yes/No
GROUP ORDERS	YES	IN	YES

The WAREHOUSE performs the *FILL ORDER* function making it definitely out of scope for the ORDER ENTRY department.

Rule 1: Verb-Object?	**Rule 2:** Transforms Data?	**Rule 3:** In Scope?	**Internal Process** Yes/No
FILL ORDER		OUT	NO

Assuming that you completed the table as suggested earlier, you should find that all of the remaining candidates fail since they are either done by the WAREHOUSE, ACCOUNTING, or CUSTOMER SERVICE making them Out of Scope for our project.

As you can see, out of the rather lengthy interview notes from Mary we actually identified only four internal processes that are part of the *ENTER ORDERS* process: *SORT MAIL, VERIFY CREDIT, VALIDATE ITEMS,* and *GROUP VALID ORDERS.*

Rule 1: Verb-Object	**Rule 2:** Transforms Data	**Rule 3:** Scope	**Internal Process** Yes/No
TRIGGER ACTION	No	Out	No
RECEIVE ORDERS, COMPLAINTS, AND PAYMENTS	No	In	No
SORT MAIL	Yes	In	Yes
VERIFY CREDIT	Yes	In	Yes
VALIDATE ITEMS	Yes	In	Yes
SEND ORDERS	No	In	No
HOLD ORDERS	No	Out	No
ACCUMULATE VALID ORDERS	No	In	No
GROUP ORDERS	Yes	In	Yes
TRANSMIT VALID ORDERS	No	In	No
FILL ORDER	??	OUT	No

A Level 2 Data Flow Diagram will show how these four internal processes transform the incoming flows to create all outgoing flows.

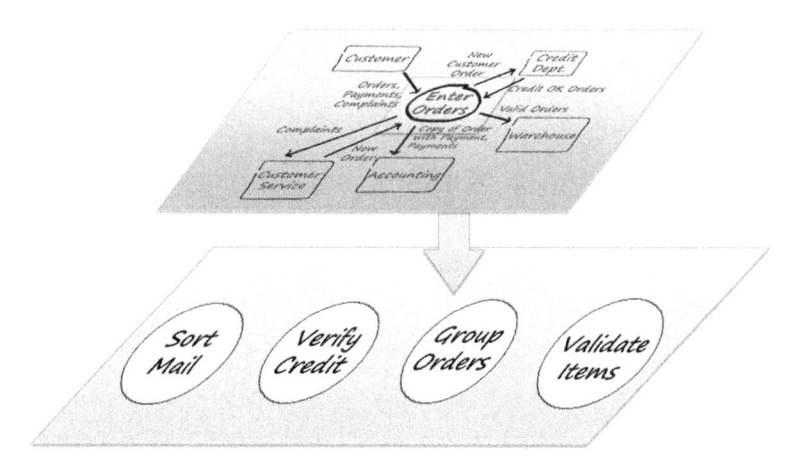

While drawing the diagram, we may discover missing flows and/or missing internal processes. That is not a bad thing; it is one of the major benefits of exploding or levelling a process.

Given that you have these 4 processes, the next step will be to depict these processes on a detail-level DFD that shows how each of them consumes and creates data within the *ENTER ORDERS* process and how they convert the incoming mail into valid orders for the warehouse.

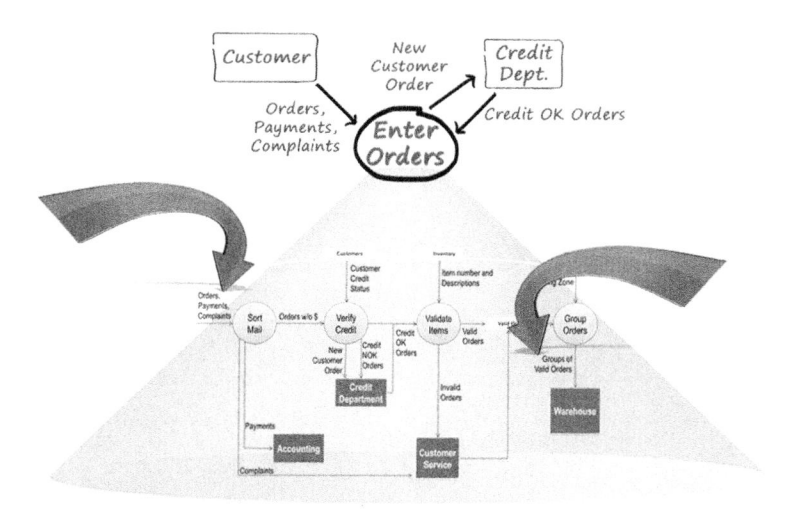

Online resources for you:

- ⇨ LECTURE 11: PROCESS MODELING
  http://faculty.washington.edu/ytan/is460/notes/LN11.pdf

- ⇨ Understanding Data Flow Diagrams
  http://ratandon.mysite.syr.edu/cis453/notes/DFD_over_Flowcharts.pdf

- ⇨ DFD Problems and Exercises Solutions
  https://keantak.files.wordpress.com/2010/09/dfd-problems-and-exercises-solutions.pdf

- ⇨ DFD Rules
  https://www.dlsweb.rmit.edu.au/toolbox/ecommerce/tbn_respak/tbn_e2/html/tbn_e2_devsol/dfds/dfdrules.htm

DRAWING A DETAIL LEVEL DFD

Questions answered in this chapter:

- What is a simple approach for drilling down into a process?
- Why do it and where can I start?
- How can I show the internal processes and flows that produce the results?

This chapter is about assembling the identified processes at the appropriate level of detail to model how these processes transform, transport, and store data.

When you draw a detailed Data Flow Diagram that includes all of the identified processes, you almost always discover "hidden" processes, flows, and data stores. That is not a failure on your part; it is one of the powerful side effects of the modeling approach.

Discovering these missing components this early in the analysis minimizes the possibility of being forced to increase the scope of your project later on to address them. The ensuing detail-level DFD is an essential tool for minimizing the risk of disconnects and missing requirements for your IT projects.

Exploding or Leveling High-Level Processes on a DFD

Looking at the Context diagram, the "Orders, Complaints, and Payments" data flow from the CUSTOMER is where it all starts. Based on the interview notes

---

Interview Notes *(Excerpt)*

The customer triggers all the action in our department. We receive an order (with or without payment), a complaint, or a payment (with or without invoice copy) from the customer. <u>These are separated</u> and the following actions take place.

---

and our list of potential internal processes, SORT MAIL appears to be the first step in the process.

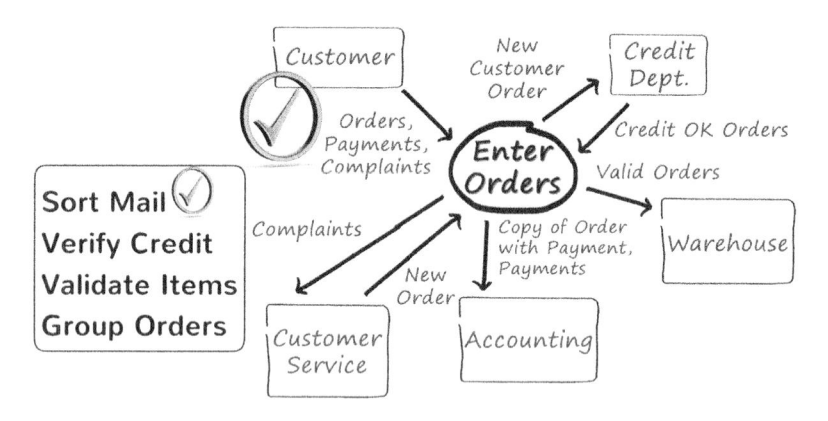

Therefore, I start my detailed diagram on the left side of a new sheet of paper with the *Orders, Complaints, and Payments* flow coming from the left into the process *SORT MAIL*.

By the way, data flow diagrams tend to grow wide as opposed to high so I suggest drawing the diagram in "Landscape" orientation. With that layout option, I am going to try to simply draw the diagram horizontally across the middle of the page, leaving space both above and below the symbols for additional information that I somehow always need.

Note that I am exploding a process *ENTER ORDERS* from a higher level diagram which clearly shows the *Orders, Complaints, and Payments* data flow coming from the external entity CUSTOMER. Technically speaking, I do not have to repeat the external entity symbol on the lower level diagram - but I will if it adds clarity.

Based on Paul's explanation of what the *SORT MAIL* process entails, I add three separate flows *Orders, Complaints, Payments* as the outcome of the process. Since my primary interest is the *Orders*, that is the data flow going out to the right of the process. The other two secondary flows come out of the lower part of the process symbol.

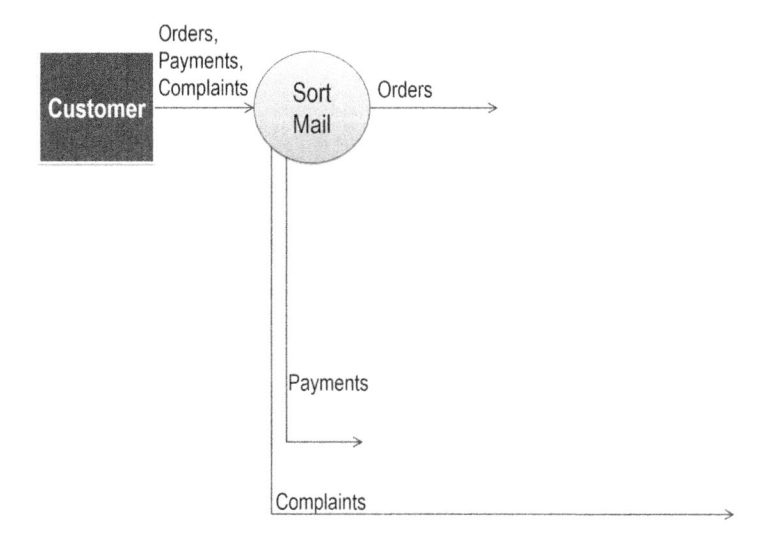

Based on the narrative,

Interview Notes *(Excerpt)*

If it is an order, we <u>verify an existing customer's credit status</u> and then we verify that the item numbers are valid by checking our inventory file. New customer's orders are sent to the credit department and held until they clear a credit check. (If half payment or more is included, that order is treated as if it were a credit order with good credit.)

the next step in the process is *VERIFY CREDIT* so I add a process with that name to the right of the *SORT MAIL* process with the *Orders* data flow coming into it from the left.

The verb "Verify" on a process model always implies two inputs. I need something to verify (in this case the customer info from the *Order*) and something to verify it against. The narrative does not state what that is but Paul explains to me that he verifies a customer's credit status by checking the **CUSTOMERS** data store.

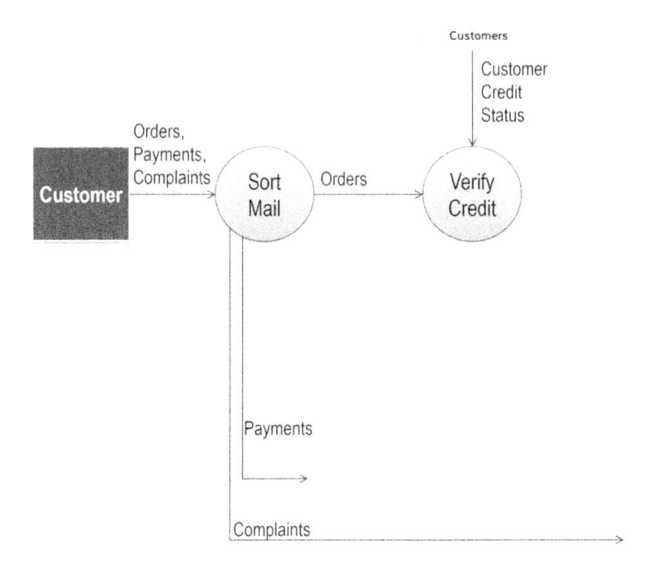

This revelation causes me to add the data store CUSTOMERS above the *VERIFY CREDIT* process and the data flow *Customer Credit Status* from CUSTOMERS to *VERIFY CREDIT*.

Drawing this forces me to ask Paul what happens if the customer is not in the **CUSTOMERS** data store? "Well, that would mean it is a new customer in which case we send the order over to the CREDIT DEPARTMENT for a credit check" Paul replies.

I represent this knowledge by adding a data flow labeled *New Customer Order* coming out of the bottom of the *VERIFY CREDIT* process. Since the flow with that name is shown on the Context Diagram going from *ENTER ORDERS* to the CREDIT DEPARTMENT, I do not have to draw the external entity CREDIT

DEPARTMENT on my detailed diagram (but I will if it adds clarity).

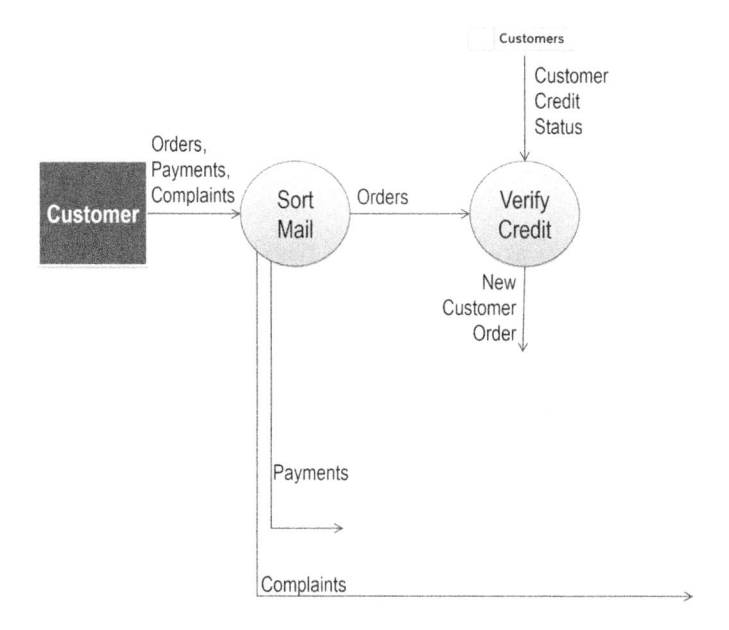

```
                                          Customers
                                             │
                                          Customer
                                          Credit
                                          Status
                    Orders,                  │
                    Payments,                ▼
                    Complaints   ┌──────┐  Orders  ┌──────┐
         ┌────────┐             │ Sort │─────────▶│Verify│
         │Customer│────────────▶│ Mail │          │Credit│
         └────────┘             └──────┘          └──────┘
                                    │                │
                                    │             New
                                    │             Customer
                                    │             Order
                                    │                ▼
                                    │
                                Payments
                                    │
                                    └─▶
                                Complaints
                                    │────────────────────▶
```

Customers with good credit go to the next process, which our narrative indicates

---

Interview Notes *(Excerpt)*

If it is an order, we verify an existing customer's credit status and then we <u>verify that the item numbers are valid by checking our inventory file.</u>

---

is the *VALIDATE ITEMS* process so I add *Credit OK Orders* coming out of the right-hand side of the *VERIFY CREDIT* process going into the left side of the new *VALIDATE ITEMS* process.

That begs the question, "What happens to customers with bad credit?" which Paul explains are also sent to the CREDIT DEPARTMENT. This adds the flow *Credit NOK Orders* drawn parallel to the *New Customer Orders* flow below the process. Since both data flows are going to the CREDIT DEPARTMENT, I add that external entity to the diagram to make it visible at this level.

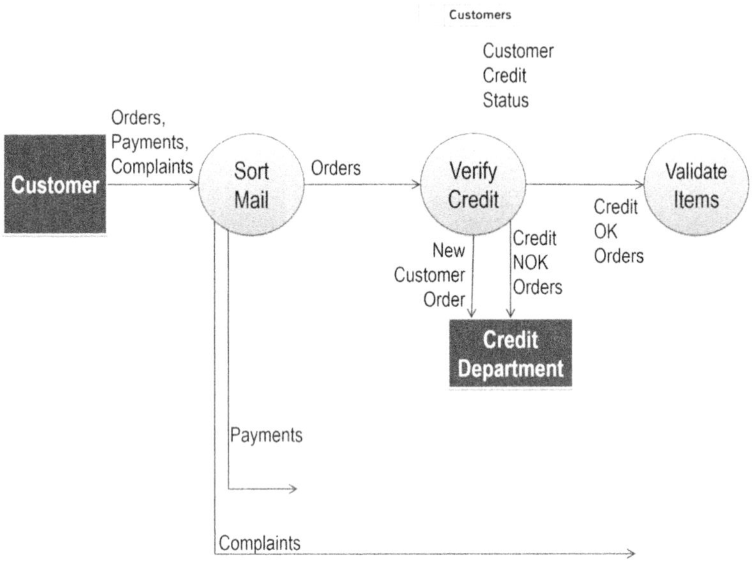
Customers
Customer
Credit
Status
Orders,
Payments,
Complaints
Customer
Sort
Mail
Orders
Verify
Credit
Validate
Items
Credit
OK
Orders
New
Customer
Order
Credit
NOK
Orders
Credit
Department
Payments
Complaints

Having done that, I refer back to the context diagram and see the *Credit OK Orders* data flow coming from the CREDIT DEPARTMENT once a new customer has cleared a credit check.

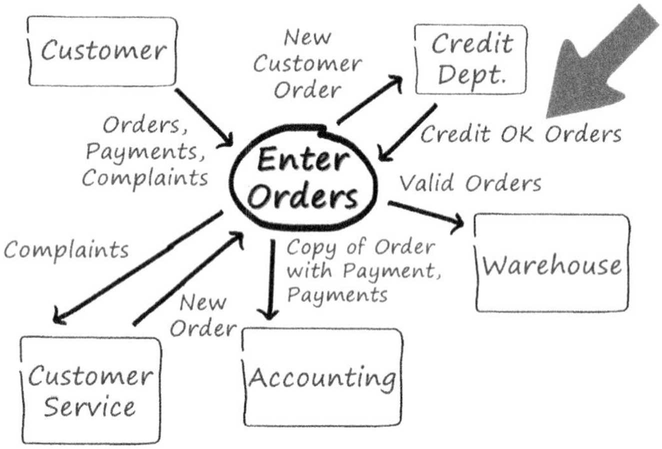
Customer
New
Customer
Order
Credit
Dept.
Orders,
Payments,
Complaints
Enter
Orders
Credit OK Orders
Valid Orders
Complaints
Copy of Order
with Payment,
Payments
Warehouse
New
Order
Customer
Service
Accounting

I ask Paul and he explains that these orders go directly into the *VALIDATE ITEMS* process the same as the *Credit OK Orders* coming from our internal *VERIFY CREDIT* process. I can simplify my diagram then by merging the two incoming flows and removing the name from the data flow from the CREDIT DEPARTMENT.

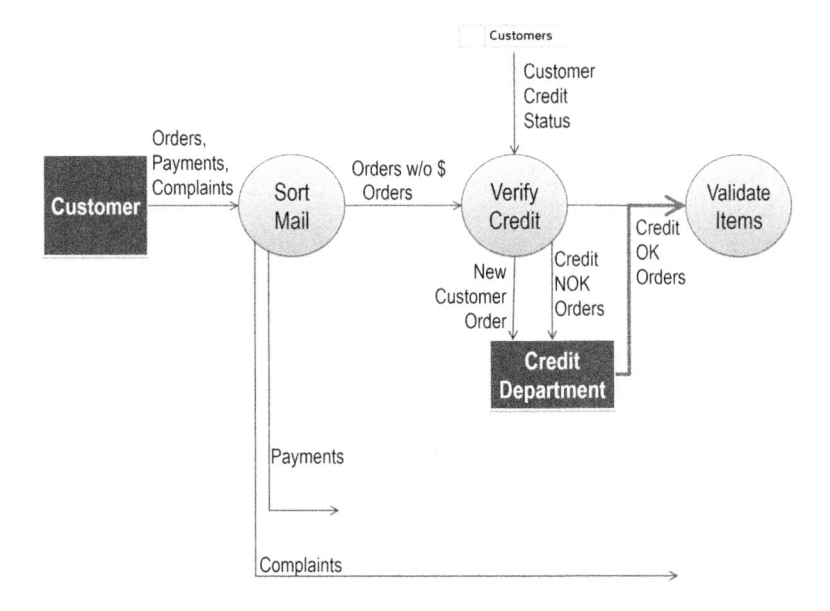

I like to keep the diagram as "clean" as possible as too much clutter confuses people. If two flows are identical, I would like to have the name of the data flow on the diagram where the two become one.

According to the narrative,

> # Interview Notes *(Excerpt)*
> If it is an order, we verify an existing customer's credit status and then we verify that the item numbers are valid by <u>checking our inventory file</u>.

the *VALIDATE ITEMS* process needs access to an **INVENTORY** file, so we add the data store symbol with that name.

When I ask Paul what they need from the **INVENTORY** file to verify the item numbers, he replies *Item Numbers and Descriptions*, so I add that flow from **INVENTORY** to *VALIDATE ITEMS*.

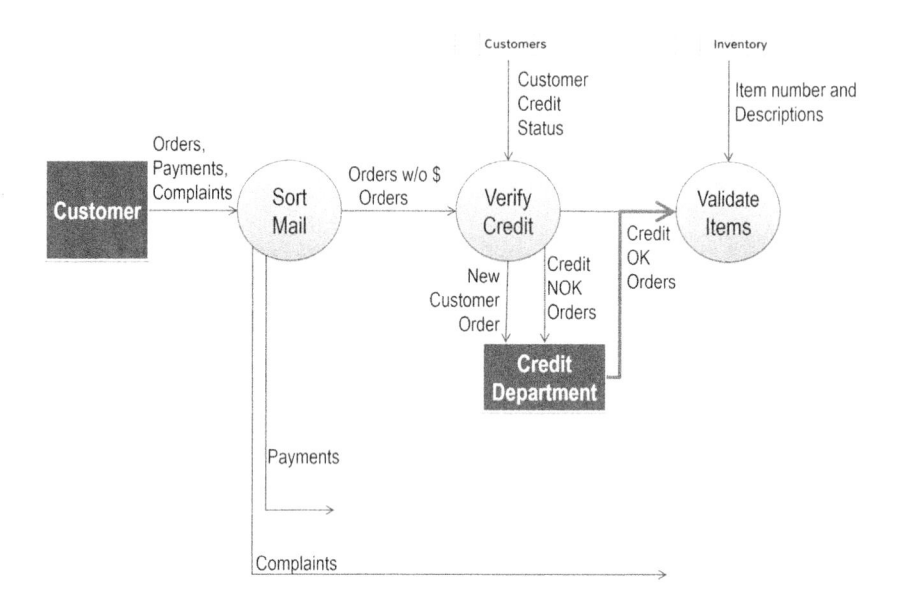

[Diagram: Data Flow Diagram showing Customer → Sort Mail → Verify Credit → Validate Items, with Customers (Customer Credit Status) and Inventory (Item number and Descriptions) as external data sources. Credit NOK Orders flow to Credit Department; New Customer Order also flows to Credit Department. Payments and Complaints flow out from Sort Mail.]

The action "validate" is just like verify" in that there will always be two possible outcomes, a good and a bad. Orders on which all item numbers are valid are called *Valid Orders* and these are accumulated - which is not a legitimate internal process but implies a data store. I add the data flow *Valid Orders* going out the right side of *VALIDATE ITEMS* into a new data store with the same name.

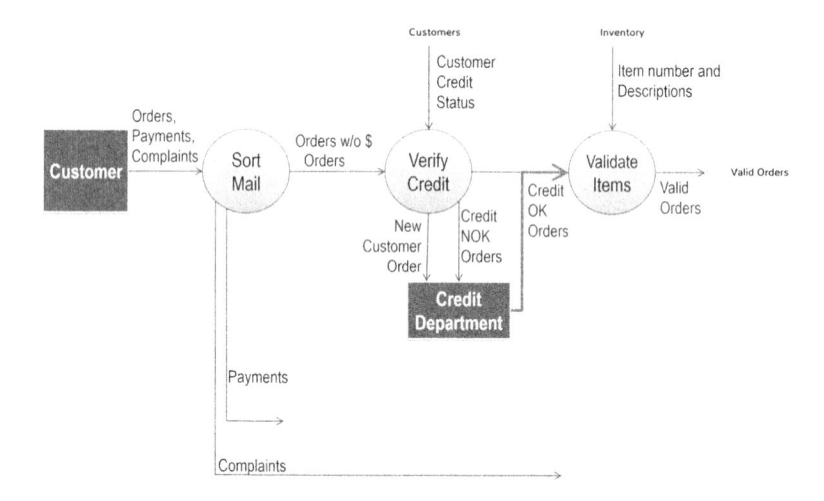

[Diagram: Updated DFD — same as above but now with Valid Orders data flow exiting Validate Items to a Valid Orders data store on the right.]

Another convention of DFD's states that if the data flow going into a data store has the same name as the data store itself, I do not have to name the data flow as it is self-evident. Removing the name from the flow allows me to shorten the arrow and move the data store VALID ORDERS closer to *VALIDATE ITEMS*, which frees up space for one more process.

First, however, I have to ask Paul what happens if there is a mismatch between an item number and description on the order and the item number and description on the **INVENTORY** file.

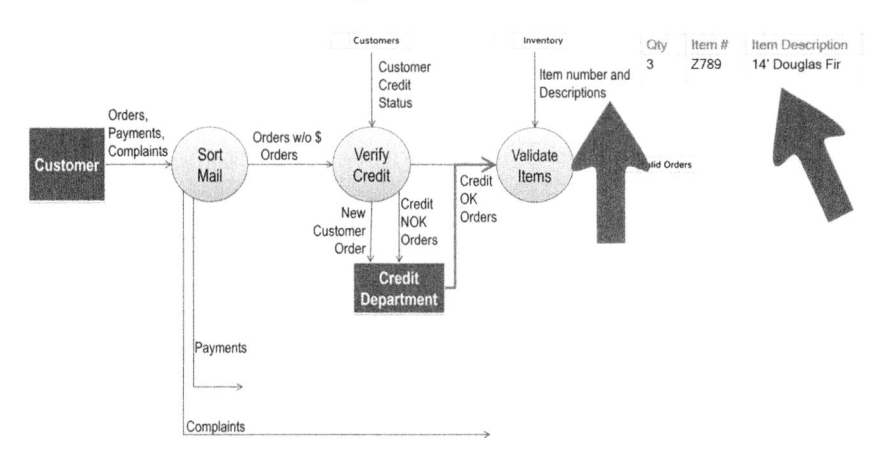

He replies that would make it an *Invalid Order* which they send to CUSTOMER SERVICE so they can contact the customer to clarify exactly what the customer intended to order. Since this revelation is new to me, I add the external CUSTOMER SERVICE below the *VALIDATE ITEMS* process as the recipient of the *Complaints* flow and add the data flow *Invalid Orders* coming from *VALIDATE ITEMS* to CUSTOMER SERVICE.

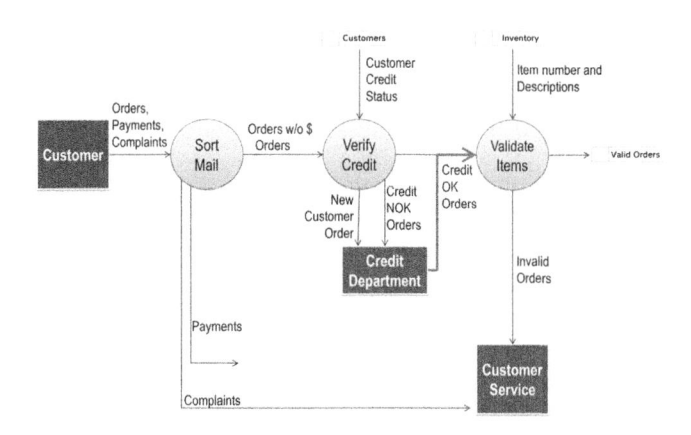

As always when I discover a new flow to an external, I need to ask the follow-on question, "Do you get anything back?"

"Sure, we get a *Valid Order* back from CUSTOMER SERVICE," Paul replies.

"And what do you do with that *Valid Order*?"

"It goes directly into the **VALID ORDERS** pile just like those orders that passed the *VALIDATE ITEM* test."

This statement adds the flow from CUSTOMER SERVICE to the data store **VALID ORDERS**. Again, since the data flow and the data store have the same name, I do not put the name on the data flow.

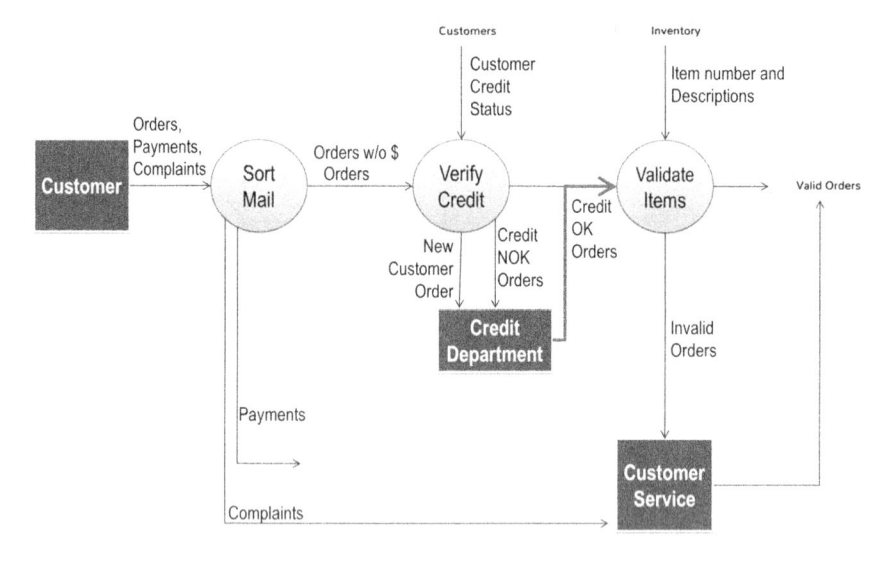

The final internal process on our list of candidates is GROUP ORDERS and the narrative confirms

Interview Notes *(Excerpt)*

<u>Valid orders</u> are accumulated and <u>grouped</u> into shipping zones.

that valid orders are "grouped into shipping zones", so I add a process

GROUP ORDERS to the diagram and add a data flow coming from the ***VALID ORDERS*** data store.

My discussion with Paul reveals that ***SHIPPING ZONES*** is a data store, which I add above the process *GROUP ORDERS* and connect the two with a data flow down to the process.

The phrase "transmitted to the warehouse"

Interview Notes *(Excerpt)*

Valid orders are accumulated and grouped into shipping zones and <u>transmitted to the warehouse</u> to be filled.

---

represents a flow from the *GROUP ORDERS* process to the WAREHOUSE.

Logically, we name the data flow Groups of Valid Orders to indicate that both the validation and grouping processes are complete. As per convention, I can either put the WAREHOUSE entity on the diagram or leave it off, as it is obvious on the context diagram.

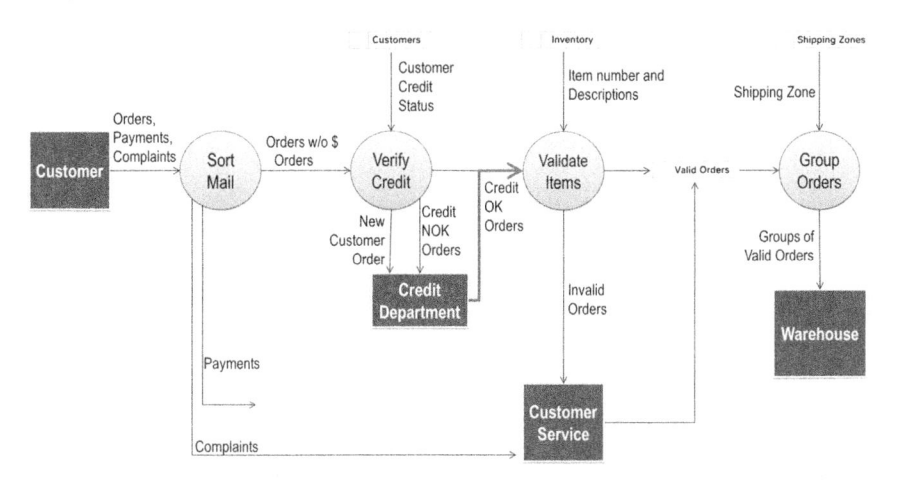

The next sentences in the interview notes from Mary describe what the WAREHOUSE then does with the order. The WAREHOUSE might be of interest if I decide to create a data flow diagram of the order fulfillment process, but in that case, I would really have to talk to someone in the WAREHOUSE to make sure I understand that process. Since the WAREHOUSE is an external entity, I do not have to worry about that for this project.

At this point, we have used all of the internal processes we identified in our initial analysis of the interview notes. Looking at the diagram, I notice that every flow leaving one of the internal processes goes to an external entity at this level with the exception of the *Payments* flow, so I add ACCOUNTING to the diagram to make it consistent.

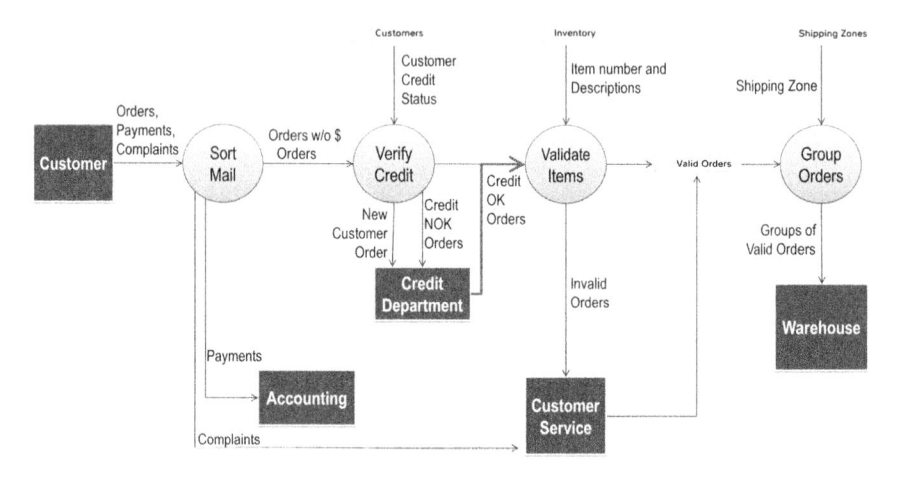

Voila, we now have a first cut data flow diagram of how the *ENTER ORDERS* process works. The only question is, how can we confirm that it is complete?

Online resources for you:

- ⇨ Data Flow Diagram (DFD)s: An Agile Introduction
  http://www.agilemodeling.com/artifacts/dataFlowDiagram.htm

- ⇨ Elements of Data Flow Diagrams
  https://www.cs.uct.ac.za/mit_notes/SE/Jul2009/html/ch03s06.html

- ⇨ How to Draw a Data Flow Diagram
  https://www.youtube.com/watch?v=KA4rRnihLII

- ⇨ Example of a Data Flow Diagram (Level 0)
  https://www.youtube.com/watch?v=zoXLU86ohmw

- ⇨ Data Flows: Common DFD Mistakes
  http://faculty.babson.edu/dewire/Readings/dfdmistk.htm

BALANCING THE LEVELS ENSURES COMPLETENESS

Questions answered in this chapter:

- What does balancing a Data Flow Diagram mean?
- What is the business value of balancing?
- What is the most efficient approach to balancing a DFD?

The payback for balancing two levels of a Data Flow Diagram can be the discovery of missing data and processes that, if not found early enough, could endanger your project. Level balancing will identify errors early in the project when it is still cheap to fix them.

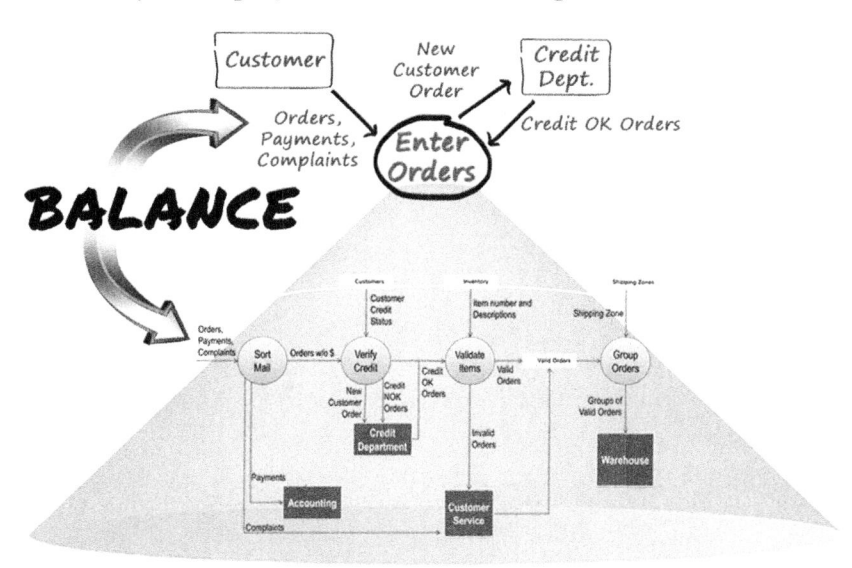

In this chapter, we explain what it means to "balance" or "level" data flow diagrams, what the business value is, and how to do it in a very simple, efficient manner. But what are you balancing and how does it work? We will start by proving that all data flows at the higher level are addressed at the lower level.

There are actually two steps to balancing the individual levels of DFDs. The first step is very simple in that I am comparing flows entering and leaving the detail level diagram with the higher level diagram. To do that, I need to be able to view the diagram containing the process I exploded and the lower-level diagram at the same time.

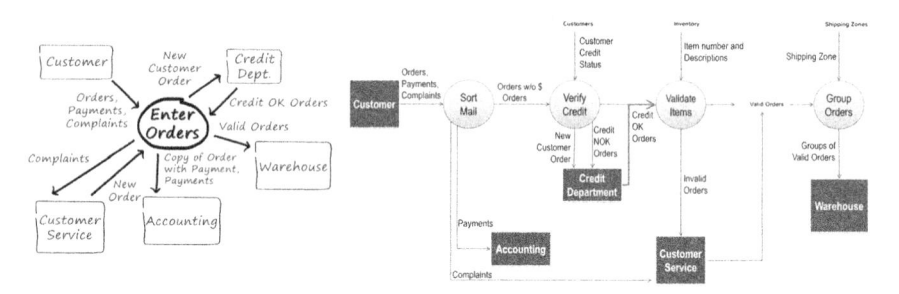

To demonstrate the balancing process in real life, we are going to use the context-level diagram of the ENTER ORDERS process and the lower-level diagram. If you remember, we developed both diagrams working with Mary, the Department Manager of the Order Entry department, and Paul, an Order Entry Clerk that reports to Mary.

Balancing Data Flows from the Higher to the Lower Level

In our example, we exploded the *ENTER ORDERS* process from the context diagram. If I now compare the exploded version with the context version, logic dictates that all flows going into or coming out of the *ENTER ORDERS* process on the Context Diagram have to show up on the exploded version going into or coming from one of the more detailed processes at that level and vice versa.

I find it simplest to balance starting at the upper level and comparing flows clockwise from that diagram to make sure they all appear on the lower level. I check the flows off on both diagrams as I go to have a visible trail and ensure that I am not missing anything.

Looking at the context diagram, I see *Orders, Payments, Complaints* coming from customer into *ENTER ORDERS*. I see the same flow on the detailed view coming from CUSTOMER into SORT MAIL. These flows are the same; therefore, I put a checkmark on them on each diagram.

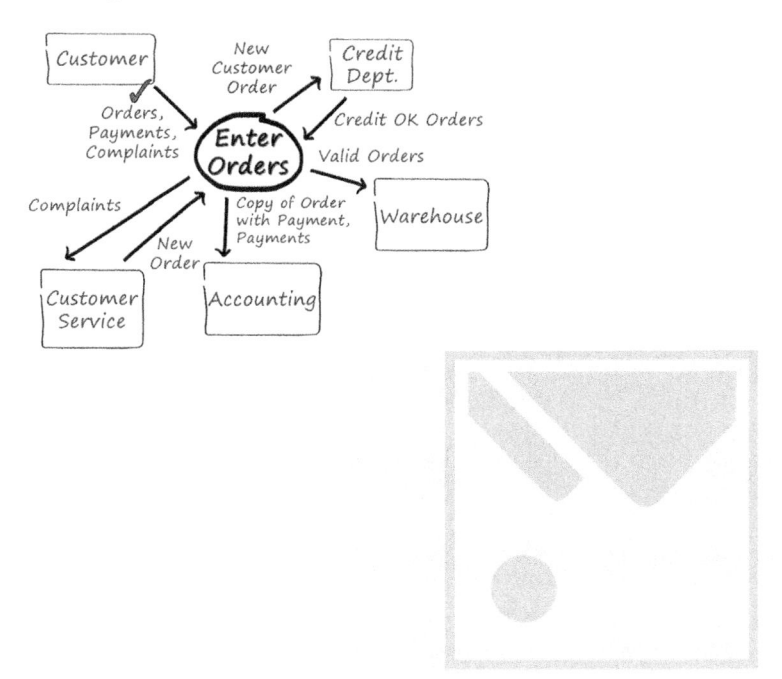

Continuing clockwise around *ENTER ORDERS* on the Context Level diagram, I see a *New Customer Order* going to the CREDIT DEPARTMENT. I see the same flow in the same direction on the lower level diagram, so I check those off. I also see matching *Credit OK Orders* coming back from the CREDIT DEPARTMENT and can check them off as well.

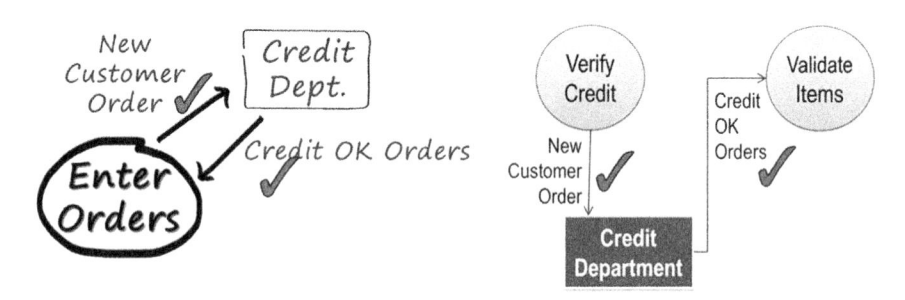

Next I see *Valid Orders* going from *ENTER ORDERS* to the WAREHOUSE. On the detailed diagram, I see *Groups of Valid Orders* going to the WAREHOUSE. After confirming with Paul that that is the only data flow to the warehouse, I would like to remove the discrepancy to avoid misinterpretation. Since the detailed level is more specific, I change the context diagram to read *Groups of Valid Orders* and check both flows off.

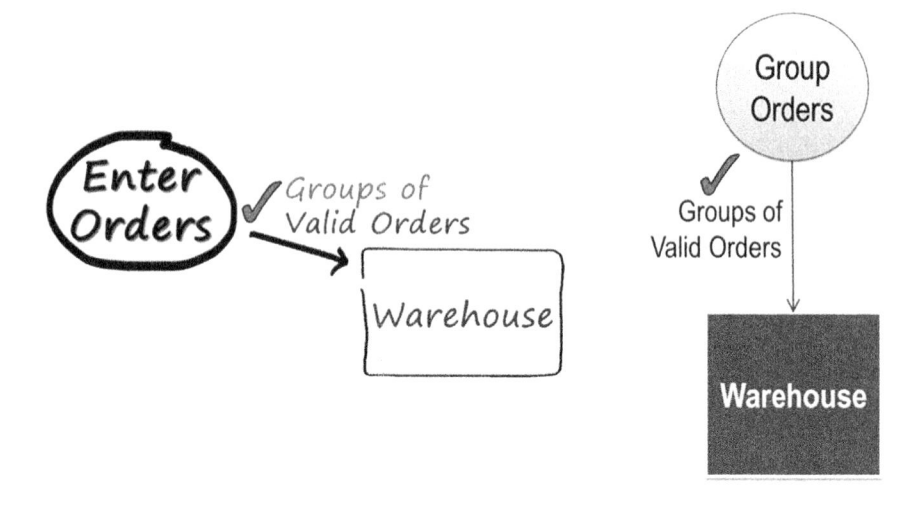

On the context diagram, the next flow out of *ENTER ORDERS* is the *Copy of Order with Payment, Payments* being sent to ACCOUNTING.

On the detail level I see *Payments* going from SORT MAIL to ACCOUNTING, so I can check off that part of the flow, but what about the other half? It appears that we missed something.

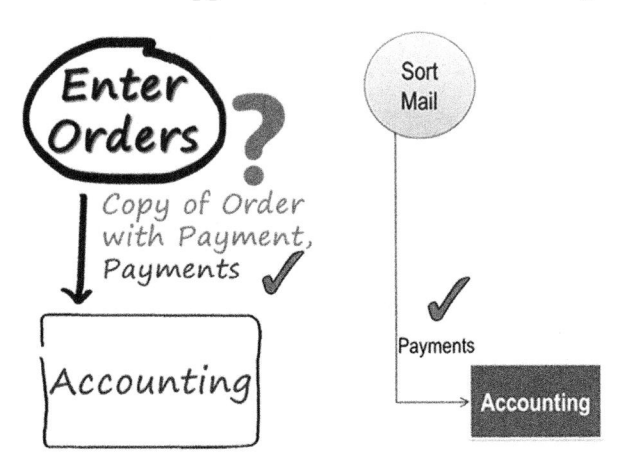

I ask Paul where the *Copy of Order with Payment* comes from and he explains that ACCOUNTING requested a copy of any order that has an attached payment. As a result, while they sort the mail, they separate orders with payment from orders without payment.

Once they are done sorting, they go through the stack with attached payments, remove attached checks from orders, make a physical copy of that order, attach the check to the copy, and put the copy of the order with the attached check on the stack of payments destined for ACCOUNTING.

If the attached payment is at least half of the total order price, the original order is stamped "Credit OK" and sent directly to the VALIDATE ITEMS process, bypassing the VERIFY CREDIT process.

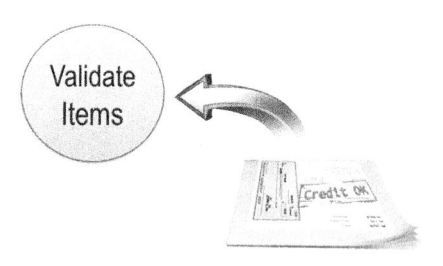

This additional information creates a problem. Obviously, we missed this little nuance in our original analysis, so we have no choice but to correct the lower level diagram to reflect the newly discovered facts.

We add a process *COPY ORDERS w/$* between *SORT MAIL* and ACCOUNTING. We add a flow *Orders w/$* from SORT MAIL to COPY ORDERS *w/$* and then add the outgoing flows *Copied Orders w/$* to ACCOUNTING, *Original Order* to *VERIFY CREDIT*, and *Credit OK ORDERS* flow to the VALIDATE ITEMS process. I have to change the Order flow between *SORT MAIL* and *VERIFY CREDIT* to read *Orders w/o $*. In addition, I change the context diagram flow *Copy of Order with Payment, Payments* to read *Copied Orders W/$, Payments* and check matching flows off on both diagrams.

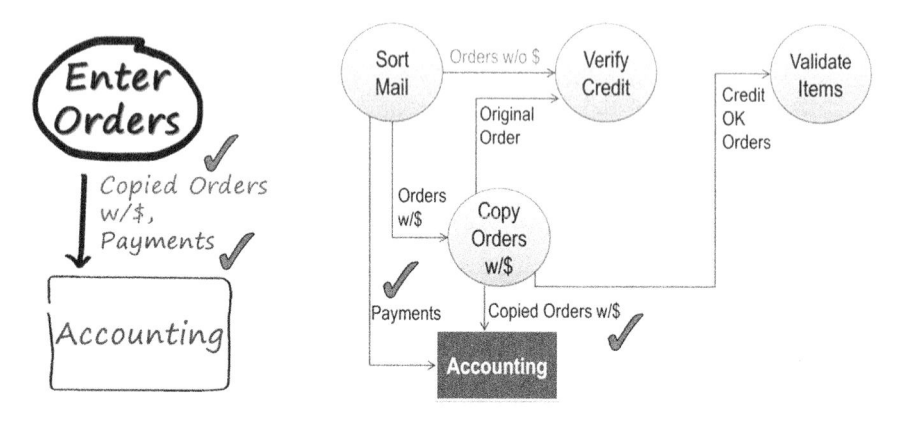

That is a great example of how exploding and leveling a data flow diagram can identify a missing process.

Back to the context diagram, I see a *New Order* coming in from CUSTOMER SERVICE. On the detail view, I have a *Valid Order* and a *Credit OK Order* both coming from CUSTOMER SERVICE.

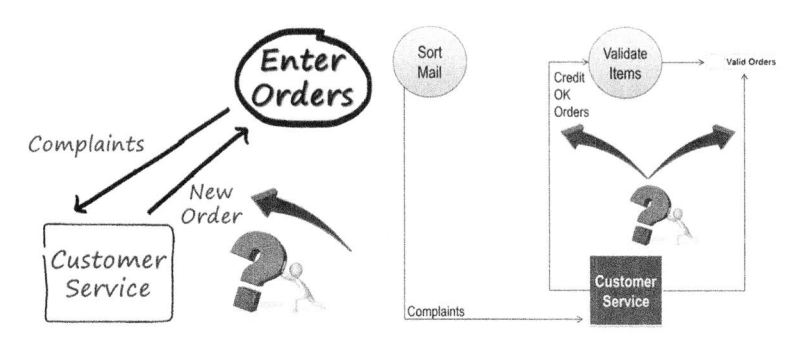

Which is the *New Order*? Paul explains that the *New Order* is one that CUSTOMER SERVICE creates in response to a complaint. It is considered a *Credit OK Order* by the Order Entry Department and they just check the item numbers, so I change the *New Order* flow on the context diagram to read *Credit OK Order* and mark those two flows off.

Note, I can only mark the *Credit OK Order* from CUSTOMER SERVICE off on the detailed diagram although I have three other flows on that diagram that are all named *Credit OK Orders*. I also mark the matching flows *Complaints* going from ENTER ORDERS to CUSTOMER SERVICE on both diagrams.

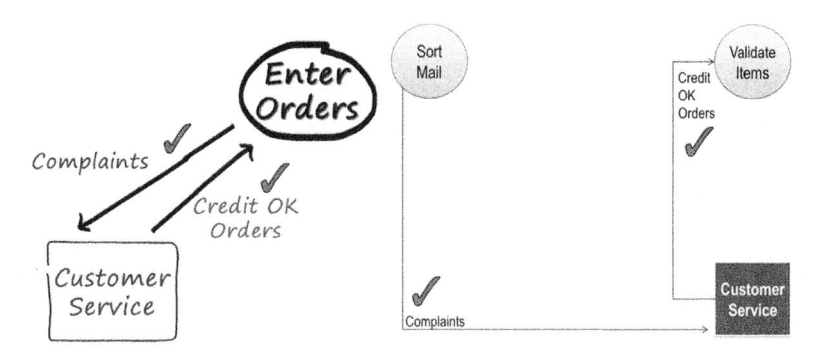

Having completed that step, I am satisfied that all flows that are on the context diagram involving *ENTER ORDERS* are taken care of.

Balancing Data Flows from the Lower to the Higher Level

Having completed that step, I am satisfied that all flows that are on the context diagram involving *ENTER ORDERS* are taken care of.

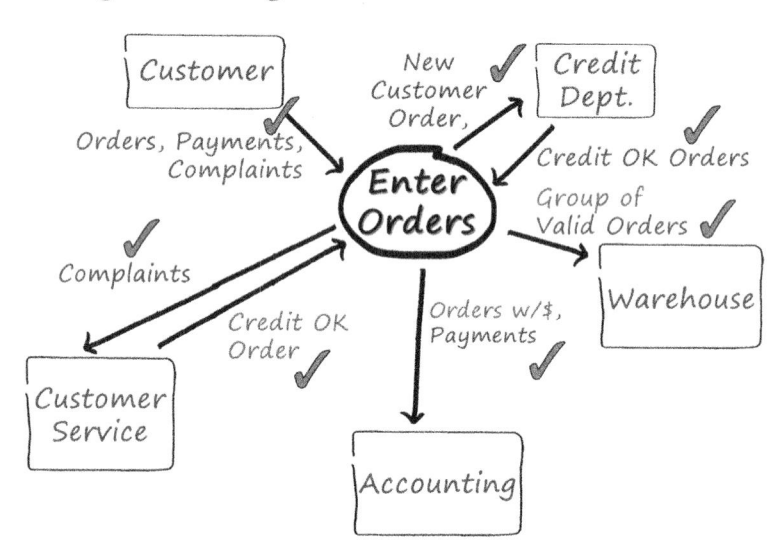

What about the opposite, have I checked off all of the flows coming into or leaving the detailed diagram? Here I am only interested in flows that are between the detailed processes and external entities and can ignore the internal flows between processes.

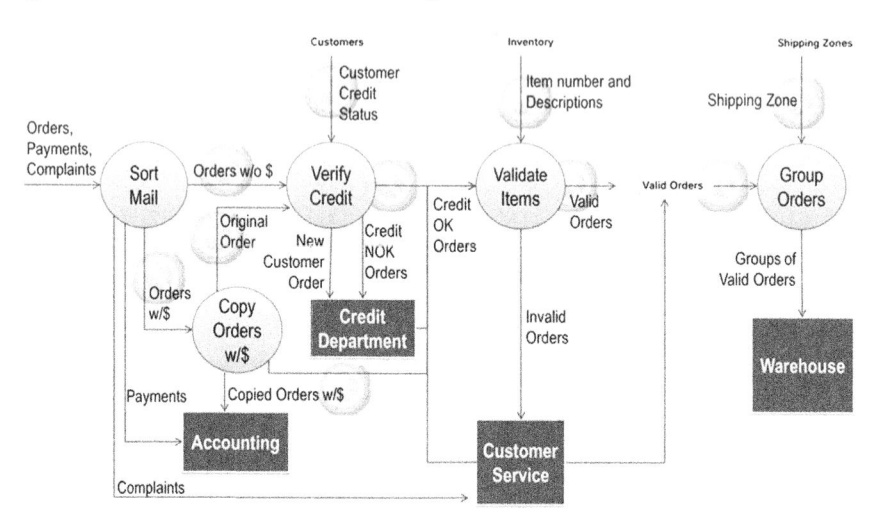

Starting with the data flow *Orders, Payments, Complaints* coming from the CUSTOMER, I proceed clockwise around the lower-level diagram to see if there are any unmatched flows. I note an *Invalid Items* data flow going to CUSTOMER SERVICE that has no match at the context level. Confirming with Paul that the detailed view is correct, I simply have to add that flow to the context diagram flowing from *ENTER ORDERS* to CUSTOMER SERVICE. I can then mark both flows as matching.

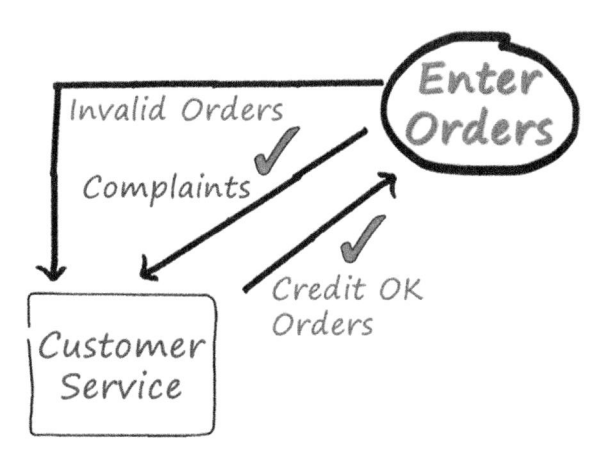

Continuing, I discover that the detailed diagram also shows CUSTOMER SERVICE sending *Valid Orders* directly into the internal data store with that name. On the context level diagram, they only send *Credit OK Orders*. Checking with Paul, I discover that *Valid Orders* from Customer Service are the corrected *Invalid Orders* they received from *VALIDATE ITEMS*. As a result, I add a separate flow *Valid Orders* from CUSTOMER SERVICE to *ENTER ORDERS* on the higher level diagram.

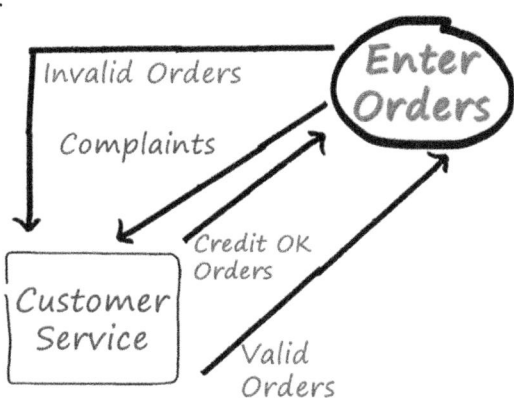

Finally, I find a *Credit NOK Order* going to the CREDIT DEPARTMENT on the lower level that is also unmatched. Again, since the flow is correct, I simply add it to the context diagram and mark it off on both diagrams.

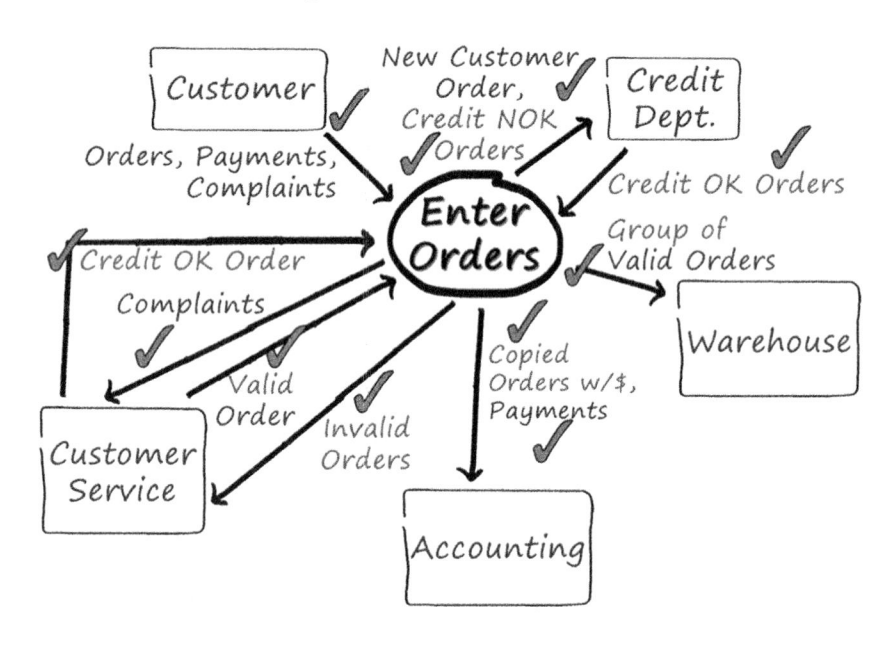

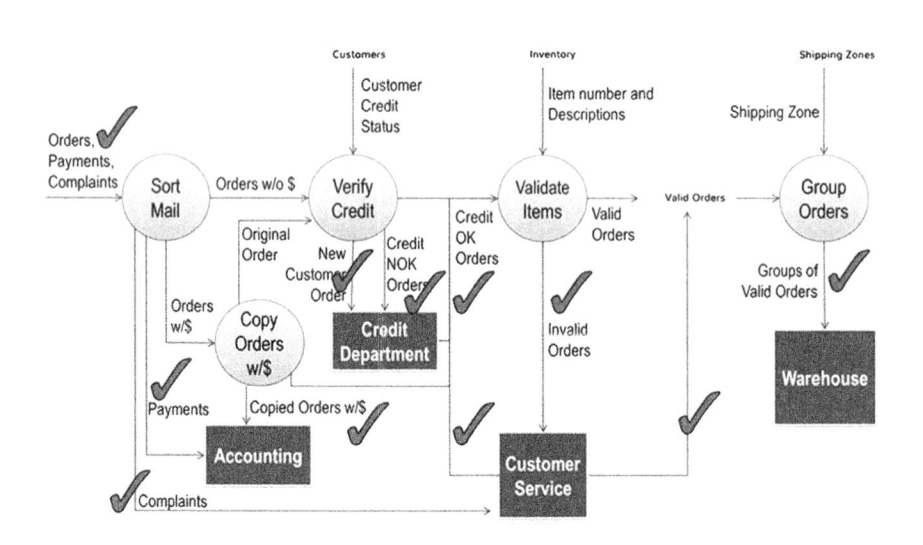

I now have a wonderfully balanced set of two diagrams, one showing the context of the project and the second detailing the *ENTER ORDERS* process. Obviously, if my project had included the WAREHOUSE or CREDIT DEPARTMENT, I would repeat the process for each respectively and would probably identify additional disconnects there.

This balancing act revealed a missing function at the lower level that is actually quite complex. Had we started defining the requirements for how we want the process to work in the future, we would have most likely ended up with an incomplete solution.

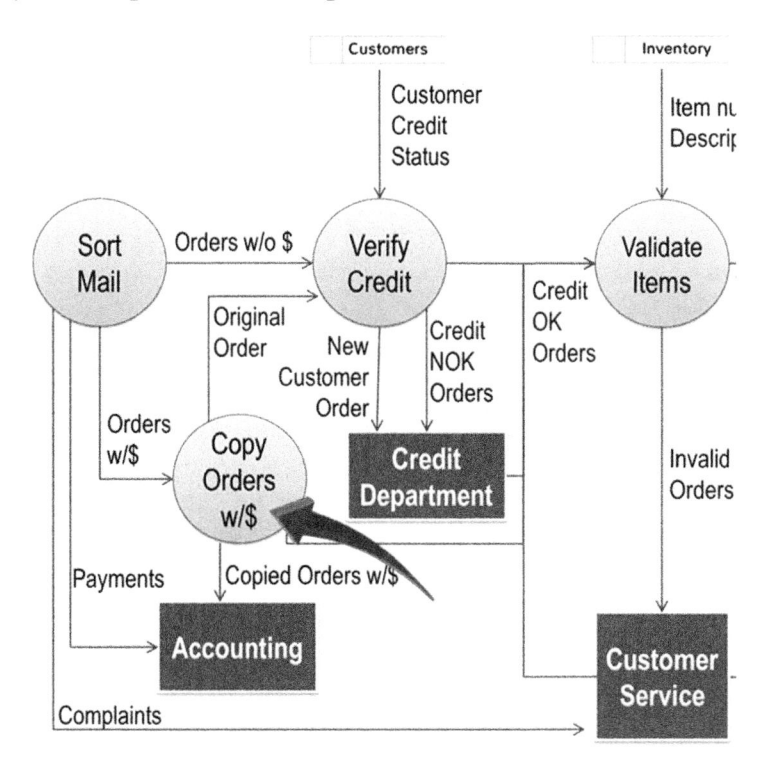

We also revealed a couple of missing flows on both levels so the act of balancing the two levels was really worthwhile.

Given that I now have a better understanding of how the ENTER ORDERS process works, the question becomes whether this level is detailed enough or if I need to go further. Remember, I can explode any process at any level on a DFD if I would like to discover and present how the process internally consumes data to produce its outcome.

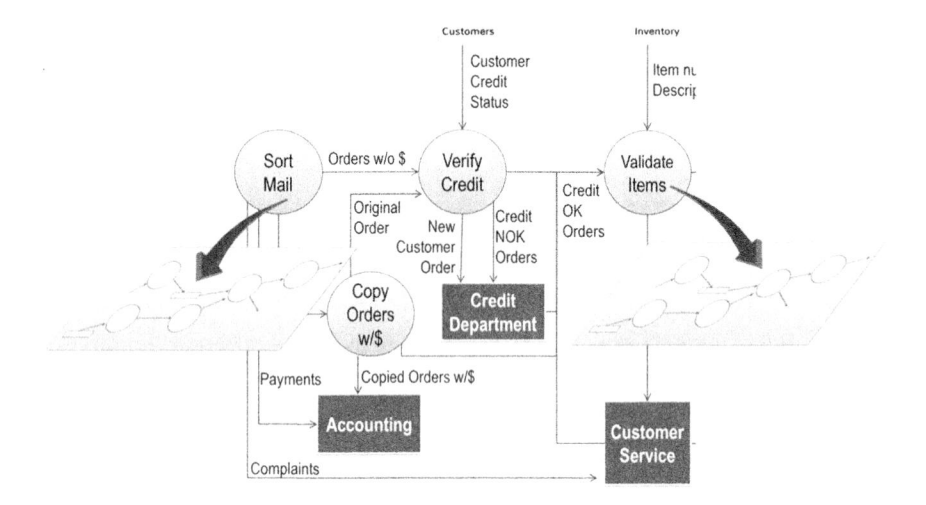

Once I feel that all relevant stakeholders understand and agree with every process on my lowest level diagrams, I consider the diagramming step complete.

Online resources for you:

⇨ Balancing Data Flow Diagrams (DFD)
https://www.youtube.com/watch?v=qyXtZvX3Lok

⇨ Decomposing diagrams into Level 2 and lower hierarchical levels
https://www.cs.uct.ac.za/mit_notes/SE/Jul2009/html/ch03s09.html

⇨ ConceptDraw How-to Guides
http://www.conceptdraw.com/diagram/data-flow-diagram-for-store-management-system

⇨ The Procedure For Producing A Data Flow Diagram
http://www.freetutes.com/systemanalysis/sa5-procedure-producing-dfd.html

⇨ QTP - What is Data Flow Diagram (DFD)?
http://qtp.blogspot.com/2010/01/data-flow-diagram-dfd.html

CREATING DETAILED PROCESS AND DATA SPECIFICATIONS

Questions answered in this chapter:

- What is the business value of process specifications?
- How can I express specifications for processes and data?
- What is "metadata" and why do you need it?

Although DFDs are a phenomenal tool for representing workflow and business processes, their focus is the transformation, flow, and storage of data. At some point in the drill-down of your processes, you reach a point of diminishing returns. Processes at this level appear to be indivisible. In the language of DFDs, these processes are "Functional Primitives" and you may need to use other tools to represent the detailed information that solution providers need.

In this chapter, we present the importance of recognizing and defining Functional Primitives using a suitable technique. In addition, we introduce the importance of capturing metadata for the individual informational components of your project.

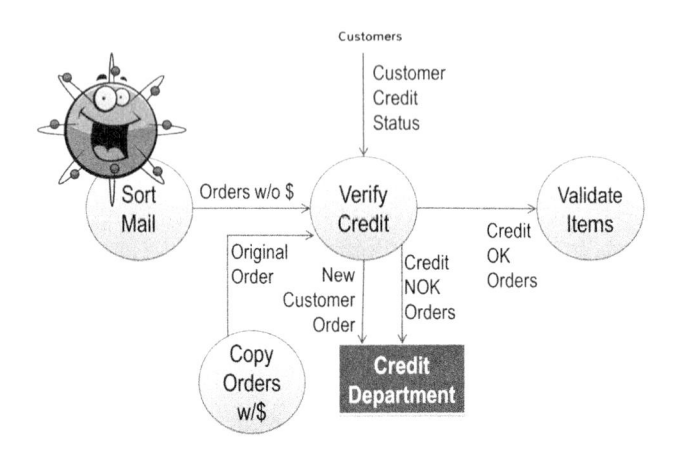

Defining Functional Primitives

At this point on your project you have created a data flow diagram, exploded complex processes to the appropriate level of detail, and balanced the two levels. You will discover that there are process details that those who will develop the solution need to know but that you cannot express using the symbols of a data flow diagram. How can you capture and communicate those details to the solution providers?

In data flow diagramming language, any process that you do not explode to a lower level of detail is called a "Functional Primitive". Functional Primitives are not good candidates for further explosion because analyzing the data flows within them would reveal nothing of value.

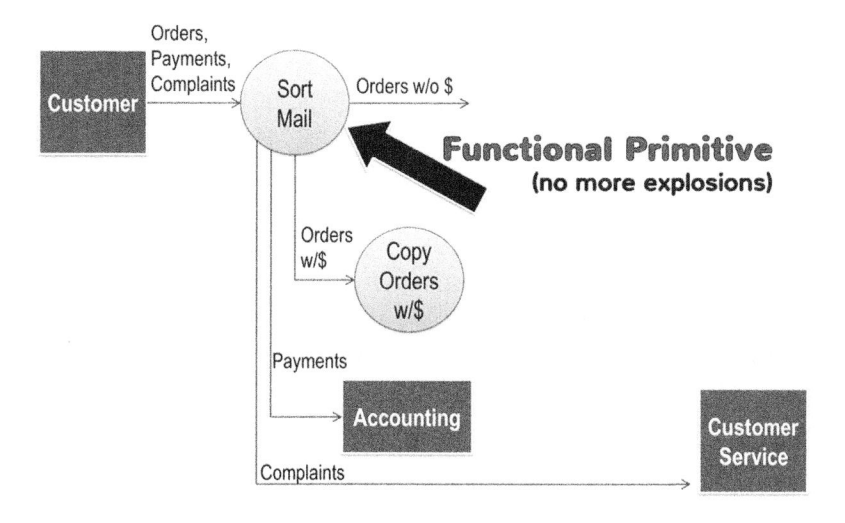

You may need to describe what happens inside a Functional Primitive using a different tool to enable a thorough analysis or to inform the downstream developers what the process really does. A description of a Functional Primitive is called a "Mini-Spec" or a "Process Specification". You have a wide range of possible tools for documenting these Specifications. To illustrate that here are several examples of how you might document the Functional Primitive *SORT MAIL*.

You could use **plain, simple English** by writing a brief description of how we *SORT MAIL*. In our example, I could write:

Mini-Specs

The mail arrives between 8am and 10am Monday through Friday. The Mail Clerk opens each envelope and separates the contents into four stacks: Orders with Payments, Orders without Payments, Payments, and Complaints. Once that is complete, the Mail Clerk processes the stack of Orders with Payments.

For each order, he carefully separates the check from the order without damaging either, makes a copy of the order, staples the check to the copy, and adds the copy with check attached to the stack of Payments destined for ACCOUNTING. If the amount of payment exceeds 50% of the total price, he stamps the order "Credit OK" and puts it on a stack labeled "Prepaid Orders"; otherwise, he places the original order on the "Orders without Payment" stacks.

Once he has processed all "Orders with Payment", the Mail Clerk distributes the stacks to the appropriate department:

- ⇨ Original Orders stay in the Order Entry Department
- ⇨ Payments and Copies of Orders with Payment go to Accounting
- ⇨ Complaints go to Customer Service

If you and your target audience are comfortable with concepts such as **Pseudo Code or Structured English**, you could also write the specification thusly:

Mini-Specs

IF Item is an Order
  IF Payment is Attached
    Separate Payment from Order
    Copy Order
    Attach Payment to Copy
    Send Copy with Payment to Accounting
    IF Payment > ½ Total Price
      Stamp "Credit OK"
    END
  END
  Continue Processing
ELSE IF Item Is Complaint
  Send to Customer Service
ELSE IF Item is Payment
  Send to Accounting
END

If the process is primarily a decision-making process and your target audience is comfortable with them, you can also use a Decision Table (also called "Truth Tables"). To create a Decision Table, open a spreadsheet, and write down each potential action as a column header starting with the second column. Our column headers for *SORT MAIL* will be:

- ⇨ Column 2: Remove check, copy order, attach check to copy
- ⇨ Column 3: Add copy to Accounting stack
- ⇨ Column 4: Add payment to Accounting stack
- ⇨ Column 5: Add order to Verify Credit stack
- ⇨ Column 6: Add order to Validate Items stack
- ⇨ Column 7: Add complaints to Customer Service stack

Starting with the second row, write down a condition that has to be met for the actions in that row to be executed. For example, in the first cell of the second row, I write the condition "Order without payment". If that condition is met, the action will be "Add order to Verify Credit stack", which I indicate by typing an "X" into the fourth column in row 2.

The next row is for the condition "Order with >49% payment". If that condition is true, the appropriate actions are to "Remove check, copy order, attach check to copy", "Add copy to Accounting stack", and "Add order to Validate Items stack", so I add "X" in columns 2, 3, and 6.

Following this logic, the next row has the condition "Order with < 50% payment which leads to an "X" in columns 2, 3, and 5.

The condition "Payment not attached to an order" in row 5 simply gets an "X" in column 4 and the condition Complaint gets an "X" in column 7.

On the following page is the finalized Decision Table for *SORT MAIL*:

Data Flow Diagrams - *Simply Put!*

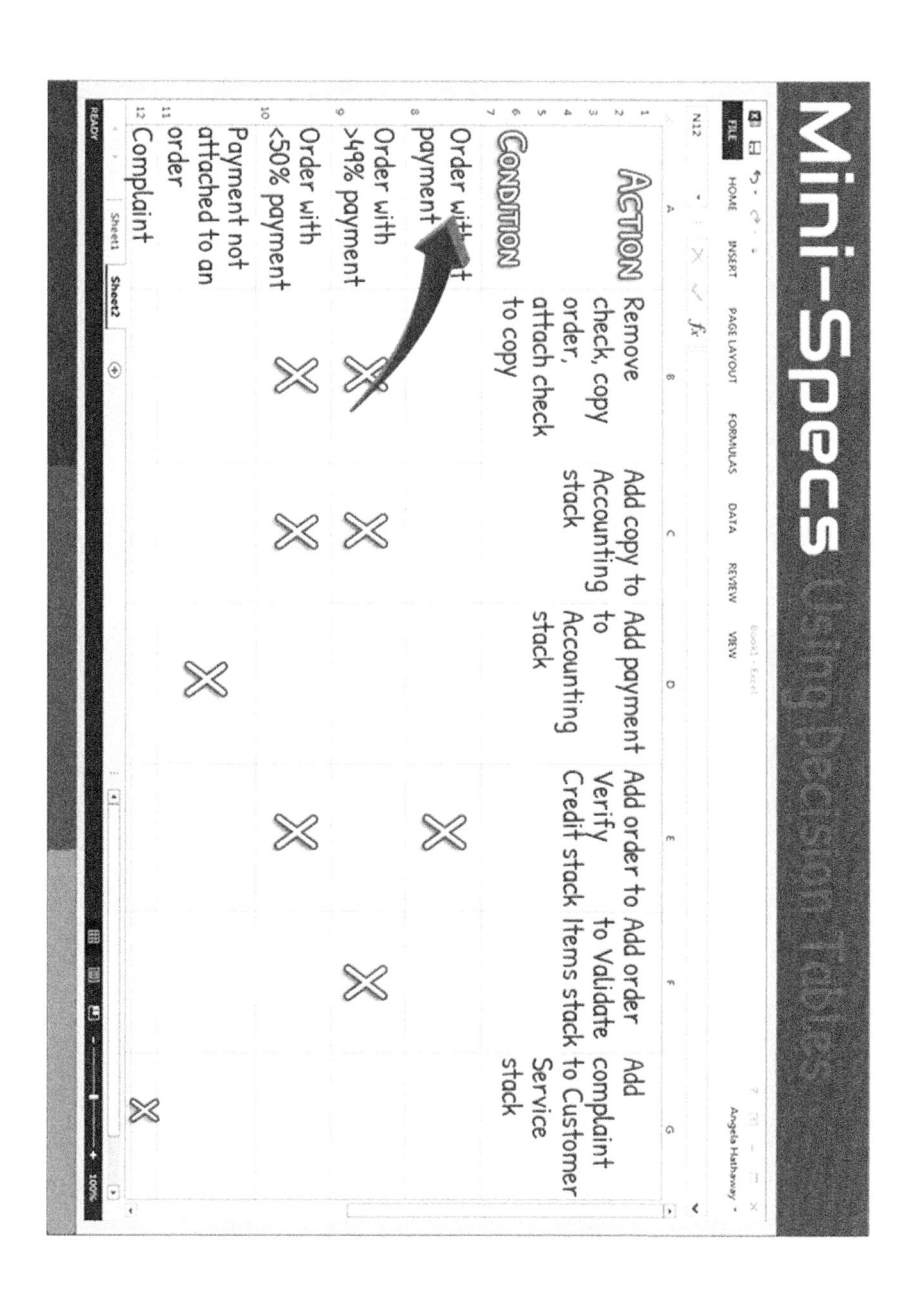

	Condition / Action						
7	**CONDITION**						
8	Order with payment	X	X				
9	Order with >49% payment	X	X		X		
10	Order with <50% payment			X		X	
11	Payment not attached to an order						X
12	Complaint						X
	ACTION	Remove check, copy order, attach check to copy	Add copy to Accounting stack	Add payment to Accounting stack	Add order to Accounting stack	Verify Credit Items stack	Add order to Validate stack	Add complaint to Customer Service stack

85

If the process involves a lot of logical branching, you might consider an Activity Diagram, an Event-Response Diagram, a System Flow Chart, or any other tool suited for depicting conditional sequences of actions.

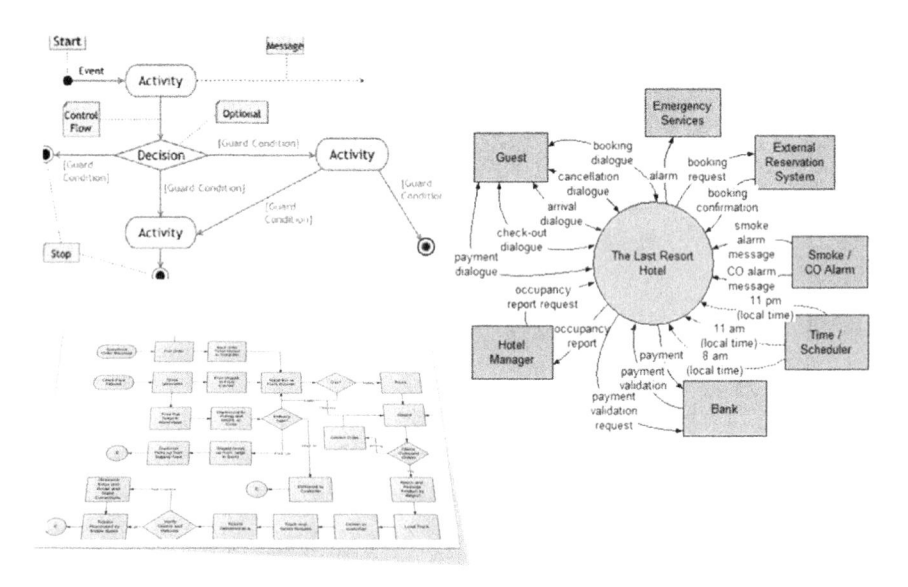

If the Functional Primitive is already automated, consider referencing existing documentation from that application. If it is not automated, check for a procedure manual describing how to do it.

Often, processes are controlled by business rules. You might consider simply listing the relevant business rules as process specifications:

Mini-Specs

Sort Mail Rules:

1. Orders with more than ½ payment are "credit OK orders"
2. Checks will be forwarded to accounting for immediate deposit
3. Complaints will be forwarded to Customer Service

Given the state of technology today, you can use your smart phone to make a video showing the people performing the process. The key here is that you have many options for capturing and expressing what a Functional Primitive does and these options far exceed the scope of this publication.

Each of the presented examples contain the same information about the SORT MAIL process. As the one wearing the BA hat, you have to pick the mode of presentation that is suitable for the process it defines and that you and your target audience both understand.

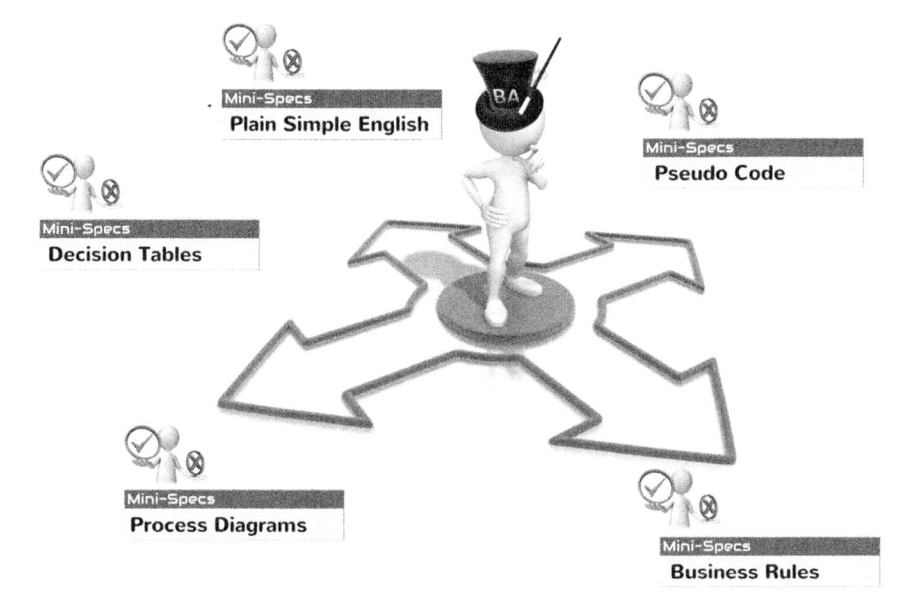

Capturing Metadata for Critical Business Data Elements

The other component of a data flow diagram is the data. Recognize that every arrow on a Data Flow Diagram represents data flowing from somewhere to somewhere and every data store represents data at rest. At the lowest level of detail, you need to understand exactly what data is contained within each data flow and in each data store.

Very often, problems in a process are caused by missing, incomplete, inaccurate, or untimely data. To be able to isolate data issues and to define the requirements for how a future application can avoid them, you need to know the data elements. You could consider this the equivalent of exploding a process. If you explode a data flow or data store to its lowest level of detail, you find a bunch of Data Elements.

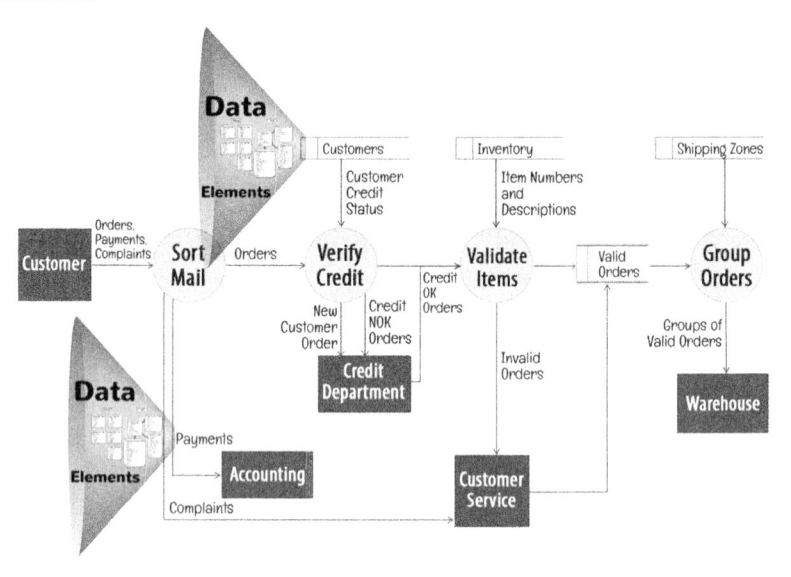

For example, the data flow *Credit OK Order* contains all of the data describing the order (customer name and address, items ordered, order date, etc.) and some indicator that this customer has good credit. To show the data on your data flow diagram, you can list all of the data elements on every data flow and every data store. Whereas this level of detail is overkill for most projects, it might be very valuable to explode one or two data flows or data stores down to the elementary level to uncover hidden problems or ensure understandable requirements. You might also consider hyperlinking the data flow or data store to a word document listing the relevant data elements.

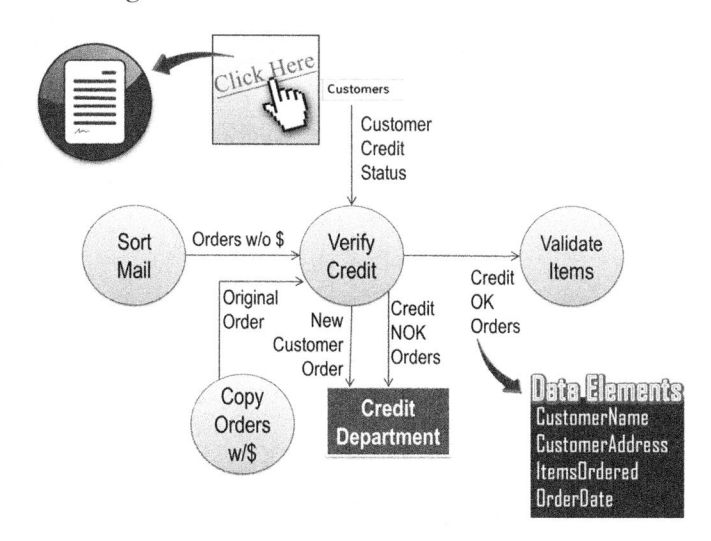

Let us look at a concrete example. This is the Order Form that our example uses:

Purchase Order

Order Date: 9/15/2014
Order Number: 141103_1966
Customer PO #: abcdefg
Customer ID: ABC12345

SHIP TO:
Fred Fuddpucker
123 Any Street
Las Vegas, NV 89011

BILL TO:
Fred Fuddpucker Jr
456 Other Street
Tampa, FL 33647

Desired Shipping Method				
FedEx				

Qty	Item #	Item Description	Unit Price	Extended Price
3	Z789	14' Douglas Fir	$63.00	$189.00
			Subtotal	$189.00
			Sales Tax	$11.34
			Total	$200.34

If I ignore the physical layout and look only at the individual data elements on the form, I get this list:

Purchase Order	
(sample purchase order form showing Order Date: 9/15/2014, Order Number: 141103_1966, Customer PO #: abcdefg, Customer ID: ABC12345, Ship To: Fred Fuddpucker, 123 Any Street, Las Vegas, NV 89011, Bill To: Fred Fuddpucker Jr, 456 Other Street, Tampa, FL 33647, Desired Shipping Method: FedEx, Qty 3, Item # Z789, Item Description 14' Douglas Fir, Unit Price $63.00, Extended Price $189.00, Subtotal $189.00, Sales Tax $11.34, Total $200.34)	*Order Date* *Order Number* *Customer PO#* *Customer ID* *Customer Name* *Ship-To Address* *Bill-To Address* *Item#* *Item Description* *Unit Price* *Quantity Ordered* *Extended Price* *Desired Shipping Method* *Sales Tax* *Total Price*

This list represents the minimum data content for every data flow on my diagram that contains the word "Order" (e.g., Orders w/$, Orders w/o $, New Customer Order, etc.). It is also the data content for the data store *Valid Orders*. Of course, that is primarily because the diagram represents a manual process involving physical order forms being moved from one process to another. There will be additional, flow-specific data elements associated with the state the order is in (with payment, without payment, new customer, etc.) but this list is my starting point.

What does the one wearing the BA hat need to communicate about each of these data elements to the solution providers so they can do their job?

Typically, they need to know what the element contains (its description), where does it come from (its source), who has the authority to change it (its owner), what kind of data does it contain (its type), how to validate its contents (data range, validation rules), etc.

Collectively, this data about each data element is called "Metadata".

Depending on the role you as the one wearing the BA hat have on the project, capturing and communicating the Metadata may or may not fall into your area of responsibility.

If you do have to capture this, I recommend creating a simple spreadsheet containing all relevant metadata about each data element, for example:

Name	Description	Source	Rights	Type	Validation	
Order Date	Date Order is received by Order Entry	Time/Date stamp	Create: Order Entry Update: N/A View: All Delete: N/A	Date	YYYYMMDD	...
Order ID	Unique Identifier for each order assigned by Order Entry Clerk	Generated by OE Clerk based on order received	Create: Order Entry Update: N/A View: All Delete: N/A	Num	Order Date + 4-digit Receipt Sequence	
Customer PO #	Purchase Order number assigned by customer	Customer Contract or Order Form	Create: Customer Update: Customer View: All Delete: Customer	A/N	None	
Customer ID	Unique identifier for each customer	Assigned by Credit Department	Create: Credit Department Update: N/A View: All Delete: N/A	Num	N/A	
...						

Obviously, the columns in the spreadsheet can be different based on your organization's needs and the project.

The key takeaway here is that solution providers need to know a ton of details about the data that the solution will manipulate. These details can be provided by the one wearing the BA hat or another role, i.e., the one wearing the Data Analyst hat. Regardless who is responsible for capturing the data requirements, the business community is responsible for defining them. These decisions should not be left to the imagination of those tasked with developing the solution or even to the one wearing the BA hat.

To summarize, at the lowest level of detail a Data Flow Diagram may need to have process specifications for every functional primitive process, a list of all data elements for every data store and data flow, and appropriate metadata for each data element. Only when you achieve that level of detail can you claim that you have a fully flushed-out data flow diagram depicting the process and relevant data for your project.

Online resources for you:

- Process Specification
  http://zimmer.csufresno.edu/~sasanr/Teaching-Material/SAD/Process-Specification/Process-Specification-Slides.pdf

- The Functional Specifications - Data Flow Diagrams
  http://www.dba-oracle.com/t_object_functional_specifications.htm

- Decision Table tutorial with examples
  https://www.youtube.com/watch?v=ED2iJXkdhCQ

- Lesson 10: Data Flow Diagrams (DFDs)
  http://nptel.ac.in/courses/Webcourse-contents/IIT%20Kharagpur/Soft%20Engg/pdf/m05L10.pdf

- Systems Analysis – Lecture 3
  http://www.uky.edu/~dsianita/695A&D/lecture3.html

- PROCESS SPECIFICATION
  http://www.nptel.ac.in/courses/106108103/pdf/Lecture_Notes/LNm6.pdf

- Process Specification Template
  https://resources.sei.cmu.edu/asset_files/Presentation/2007_017_111_436617.pdf

- Data Flow Modeling: Level 1 DFD
  http://www.sqa.org.uk/e-learning/SDM03CD/page_12.htm

- Level 2 DFDs
  http://www.sqa.org.uk/e-learning/SDM03CD/page_17.htm

- Structured Process Modeling for Systems Analysis
  http://130.18.86.27/faculty/warkentin/secure/slides/Chap09.pdf

HORIZONTAL BALANCING REVEALS MISSING DATA ELEMENTS

Questions answered in this chapter:

- What is Horizontal Balancing?
- Why do you need it?
- How do you do it?

Missing data is one of the costliest errors we can make on an IT project. The final step in the creation of a completely balanced and validated data flow diagram involves looking inside each process at each level to confirm that the process indeed needs all of the data it is accessing and that it has all of the data it needs to create the output.

We give you an easy-to-follow, step-by-step demonstration of this technique which may not be essential during the analysis, but is extremely valuable for mitigating the risk of missing data.

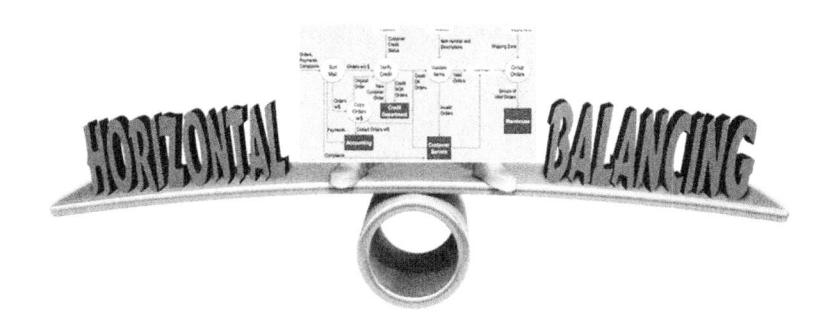

Defining and Justifying the Value of Horizontal Balancing

If you invest the time to create a data flow diagram (DFD), make sure that you are getting the most out of it. You can use the diagram to identify potentially missing data, redundant data, and possible data conflicts. We would like to introduce a technique called "Horizontal Balancing or the "Preservation of Data law. The technique can be very useful for identifying data discrepancies, inconsistencies, and conflicts which are three major contributors to IT project overruns and failures.

Based on the rules governing DFDs, a process has to transform data, meaning the data it produces has to be different than the data it consumes. Logic dictates that the data coming out of a process can only come from two possible sources:

EITHER

⇨ it comes directly via an incoming data flow

OR

⇨ the process creates it using the data it receives

A data flow can come from a data store, another process, or an external entity. Processes need algorithms or business rules to create data.

For example, the simple process "Determine Age" contains the algorithm

Age = Current Year - Birth Year
(from today's date) (Employee's Date of Birth

Algorithms and business rules in turn need data (getting the **Birth Year** requires an **Employee ID** to select the appropriate employee) which has to either come into the process from an incoming data flow or itself be created by a different algorithm or business rule. In the end, you should account for every data element the process creates and every data element it needs to create the output.

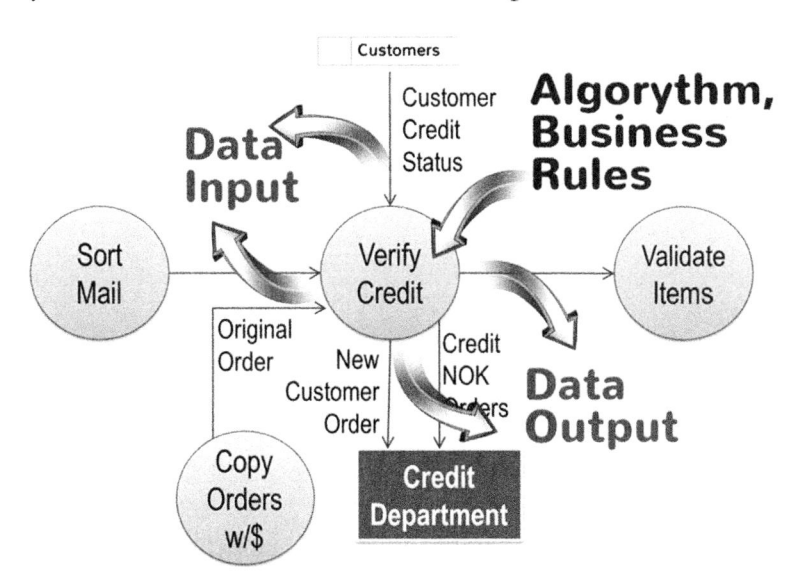

For example, the physical order form is sent from one process to the next in our example, but each process only needs specific data elements. The *VERIFY CREDIT* process only needs the **Customer ID** and/or **Customer Name** to access the **CUSTOMERS** data store. **Customer ID** and **Customer Name** are essential; all of the other data elements on the order form are irrelevant to accessing the customer data.

A Walk-through of Horizontal Balancing

I will demonstrate this concept using the *VERIFY CREDIT* process from our retail store order entry example. I will present a simulated interview with a Subject Matter Expert (SME) to explain what questions to ask and how to document and verify the results.

In this diagram, all three outgoing data flows have the word "Order" in their name because they deal with physical order forms.

In my analysis of the Order Form shown in the last chapter, I discovered it contains the data elements:

Purchase Order sample	Data Elements
Purchase Order Order Date: 9/15/2014 Order Number: 141103_1966 Customer PO #: abcdefg Customer ID: ABC12345 SHIP TO: Fred Fuddpucker, 123 Any Street, Las Vegas, NV 89011 BILL TO: Fred Fuddpucker Jr, 456 Other Street, Tampa, FL 33647 Desired Shipping Method: FedEx Qty 3 / Item # Z789 / Item Description 14' Douglas Fir / Unit Price $63.00 / Extended Price $189.00 Subtotal $189.00 Sales Tax $11.34 Total $200.34	*Order Date* *Order Number* *Customer PO#* *Customer ID* *Customer Name* *Ship-To Address* *Bill-To Address* *Item#* *Item Description* *Unit Price* *Quantity Ordered* *Extended Price* *Desired Shipping Method* *Sales Tax* *Total Price*

From the sample orders Paul, an Order Entry Clerk, provided, I also note that some have a stamp 'Attached Payment' with a dollar amount handwritten below it. Some also have a 'Credit OK' stamp and others have one stating 'Credit Check Requested'. In rifling through those stamped 'Credit Check Requested', I also find several orders in which the **Customer ID** field is blank.

I initiate Horizontal Balancing starting with the most common flow created by the process. According to Paul, that is the *Credit OK Orders* data flow going to the *VALIDATE ITEMS* process. When I ask Paul to identify the Essential Data Elements on that flow, he replies, "The only Essential Data Element in this case would be the **CreditOKIndicator** on the order. It just shows that the order is approved for further processing."

"I understand. But I also think you would need to know which order that 'Credit OK Stamp' is on, wouldn't you?"

Paul replies, "That makes sense. I guess we also need the **Order Number**, which is assigned when we sort the mail. It is added to each order by whichever of us is sorting the mail. It simply consists of the current date plus a 4-digit running number. The example I have here has order number 141103_1966 written on it by whoever sorted the mail on November 3, 2014."

Based on that information, I add **Order#, CreditOKIndicator** beneath the line labeled *Credit OK Orders* in parenthesis to indicate these are data elements.

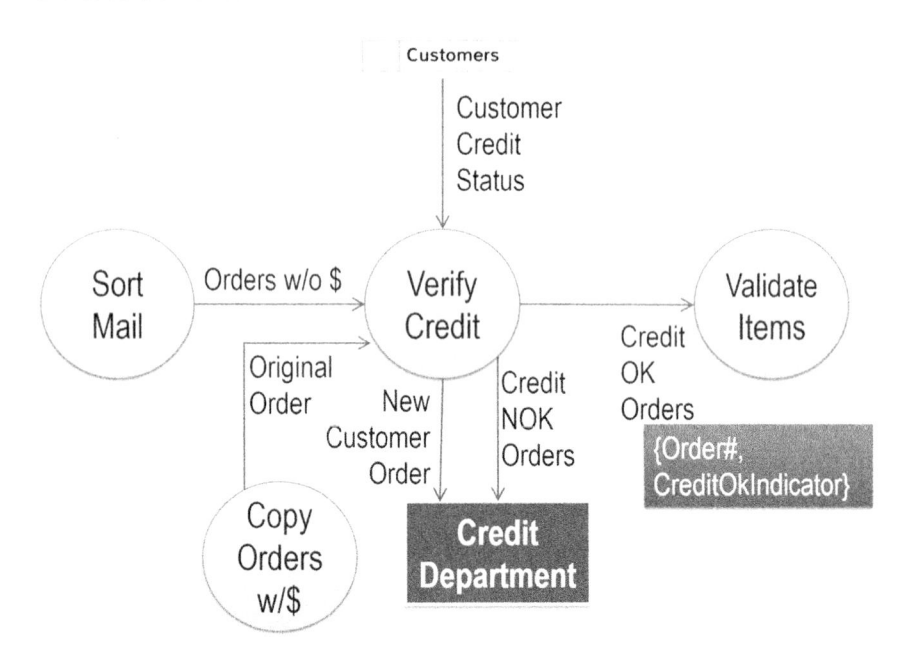

98

"OK, the next flow is the *Credit NOK Orders* being sent to the CREDIT DEPARTMENT. What is the essential information on that flow? I assume the **Order Number** and some kind of a stamp indicating the credit is not OK?"

Paul: "Those would be the ones with 'Credit Check Requested' stamped on them. That indicates it is either a new customer which we indicate by leaving the **Customer ID** blank or an existing customer who owes us from previous orders."

Purchase Order

Credit Check Requested

Order Date: 9/15/2014
Order Number: 141103_1966
Customer PO #: abcdefg
Customer ID:

SHIP TO:
Fred Fuddpucker
123 Any Street
Las Vegas, NV 89011

BILL TO:
Fred Fuddpucker Jr
456 Other Street
Tampa, FL 33647

Desired Shipping Method
FedEx

Qty	Item #	Item Description	Unit Price	Extended Price
3	Z789	14' Douglas Fir	$63.00	$189.00

	Subtotal	$189.00
	Sales Tax	$11.34
	Total	$200.34

"Makes sense. So Essential Data for the *Credit NOK Orders* data flow would be the **Order Number** and the **Check Credit Request Stamp**, right? Does the CREDIT DEPARTMENT need any other information to deal with these orders?"

"Sure, they need to know the **Total Price** on the order so they can determine whether they should OK the order and send it back to us with the 'CreditOKStamp' on it or not."

"What do they do with *Credit NOK Orders* that you send them that they do not approve?"

"You would have to ask someone in the CREDIT DEPARTMENT that. I think they send them over to CUSTOMER SERVICE to contact the customer since they are the only ones in the company who are allowed direct customer contact."

"If that's true, that would be between the CREDIT DEPARTMENT and CUSTOMER SERVICE, both of whom are out of scope for our project so we won't worry about those orders." I jot down **Order#, CheckCreditRequest Indicator, Total Price** below the *Credit NOK Orders* label.

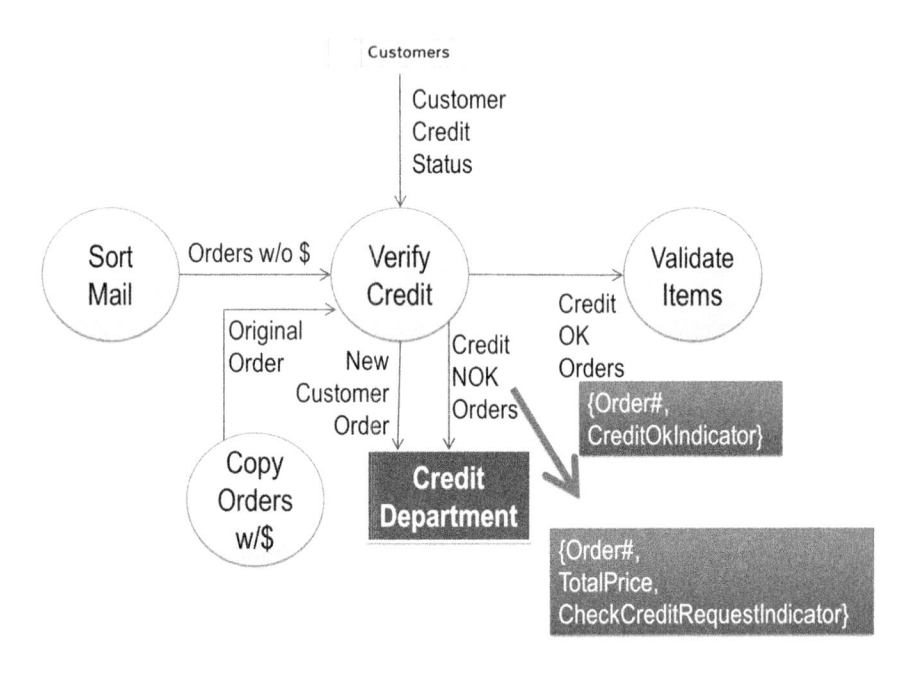

"And I guess the same is true for *New Customer Orders*, right?"

"No. An order is from a new customer if we can't match the **Customer Name** and **Bill-To Address** from the order with any customers in our **CUSTOMERS** file. Actually, if the customer provides a **Customer D**, we look for that first and if we find it in our file, we compare the **Customer Name** and **Bill-To Address** from the order to our file. If they match, then we simply look at the customer's **Credit Status** and put the respective stamp on the order.

"If the **Customer ID** on the form is blank, we have to search the alphabetical customer list to try to find the customer. If we have a customer with a matching name, we compare the **Bill-To Address** on the form with the one in our **CUSTOMERS** file. If they match, we fill in the **Customer ID** on the order. If that customer has good credit, we add the 'Credit OK stamp' to the order and put it on the stack waiting for the *VALIDATE ITEMS* process. If the customer has bad credit, we use the stamp, 'Credit Check Requested' and put it on the pile going to the CREDIT DEPARTMENT. If we can't find the customer either by the **Customer ID** or by the **Customer Name**, we stamp the 'Order Credit Check Requested' and put it on the pile going to the CREDIT DEPARTMENT."

I add the data elements **CustomerID, Customer Name, Bill-To Address,** and **Credit Status** to the data flow coming from the **CUSTOMERS** data store into the *VERIFY CREDIT* process. In addition, I add the **Customer Name, Bill-To Address, CheckCreditRequest Indicator,** and **Total Price** below the *New Customer Orders* label and ask, "Does that accurately represent what you just told me?"

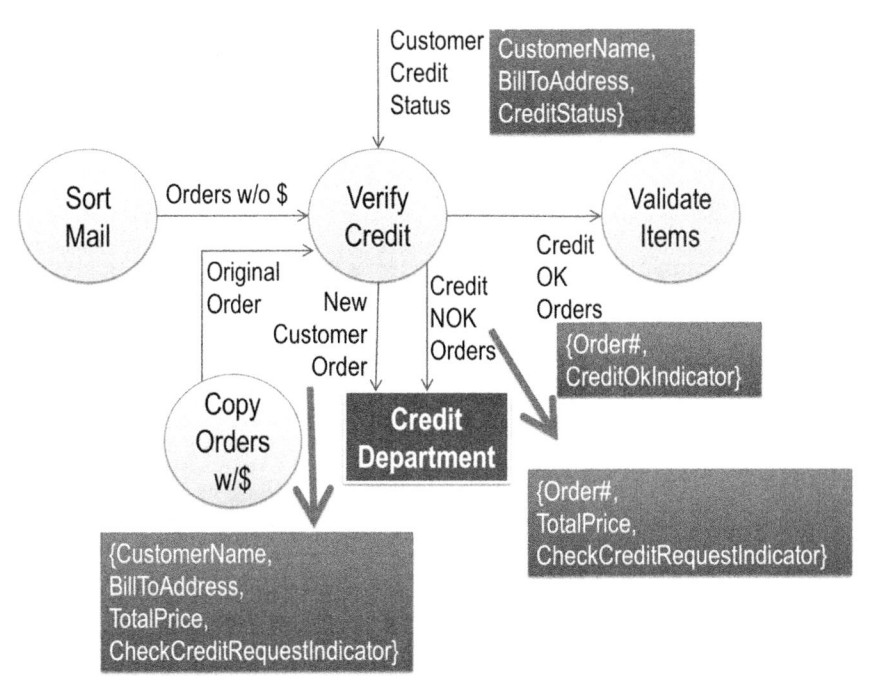

Paul replies, "I think so. I don't know whether the CREDIT DEPARTMENT needs anything else from us for a *New Customer Order*, but what you wrote down makes sense to me. I am not sure they don't need the **Ship-To Address** for the customer as well. You might want to check with them to confirm that they do not need anything else, though."

"I will certainly run this by them to see if this is all the data they need to process either a *New Customer Order* or one from a customer with bad credit. For now, we will assume that the Data Elements I listed on the diagram are the essential Data Elements on each flow coming out of the *VERIFY CREDIT* process. As I explained earlier, each of these data elements has to come into the process on one of the incoming data flows or be created in the process."

"Coming back to the primary data flow *Credit OK Orders*, you told me that the **Order#** is created in the *SORT MAIL* process, right?"

Paul replies, "Right. That's the number we have to add to make sure we can keep track of the order."

"Great!" I write **Order#** beneath the data flow labels *Orders w/o $* and *Original Order* and add, "I assume that this is true whether the order had any payment attached or not, correct?" Paul confirms my assumption.

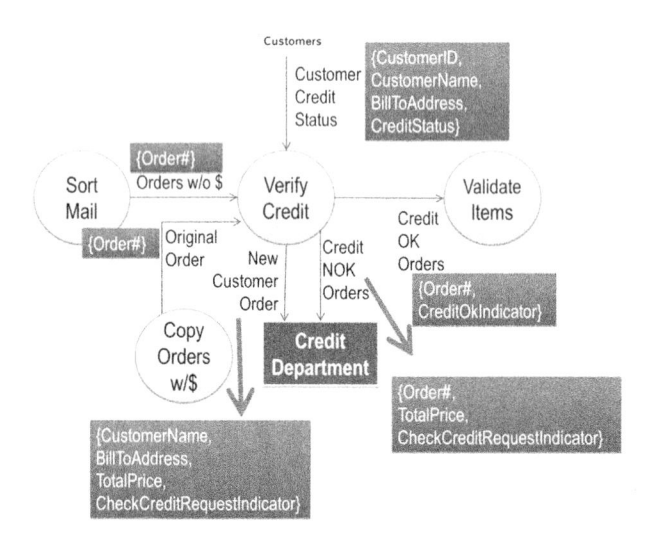

102

"Furthermore, I understood you earlier to indicate that you always get a *Customer Name*, and *Bill-to Address* from the order and sometimes you also get a *CustomerID*."

After Paul confirms, I add those Data Element names below the *Order#* on both, the *Orders w/o $* and *Original Order* data flows. I also notice that the *Total Price* is on the order form so I add it as a data element to the *Orders w/o $* and the *Original Order* data flows.

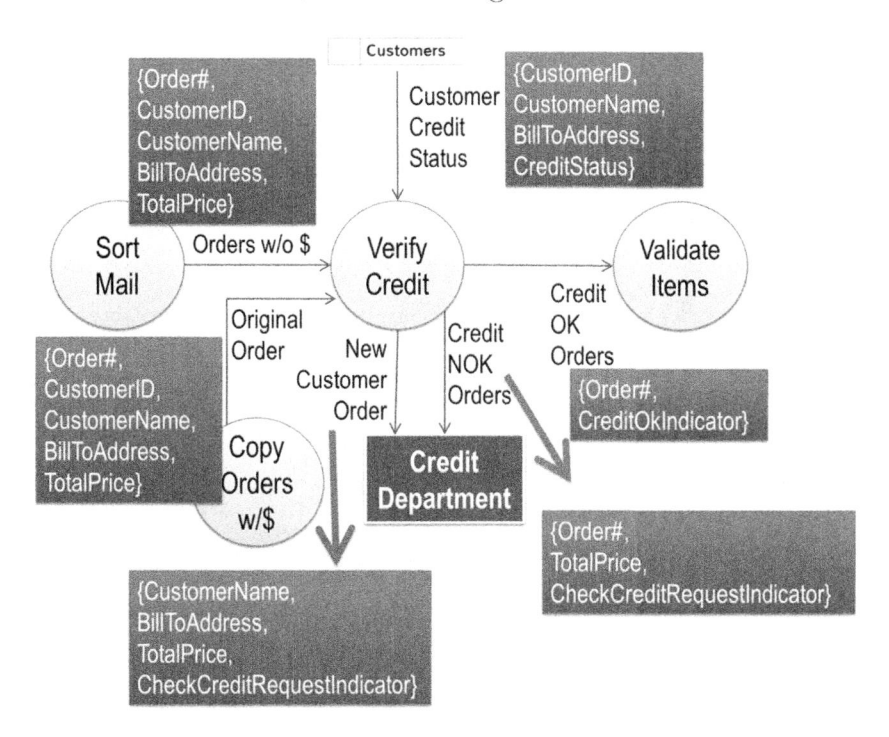

Having dealt with all outgoing and incoming flows, I now review the results with Paul. "It appears that the only data *VERIFY CREDIT* creates is the *CreditOK Indicator* or the *CheckCreditRequest Indicator*. Both of them are created based on the contents of the *Customer's Credit Status*, which is coming out of the *CUSTOMERS* File. You find the customer based on either the *CustomerID* or both *Customer Name* and *Bill-To Address*. Both of them are coming in on one of the two order data flows. Is that all correct?"

Paul agrees.

Horizontal balancing can be a hard sell for the one wearing the BA hat. It is important to impress upon the Subject Matter Experts (SMEs), however, that you are ensuring that the processes on the DFD work right.

Missing data stubbornly remains one of the most expensive errors made on IT projects. This simple technique can eliminate that problem early in the project when fixing it is still very cheap. If the problem is not identified until the developers are ready to deliver the solution, the cost of fixing it can increase by orders of magnitude.

Online resources for you:

⇨ Data Requirements - Should The Business Analyst Care?
https://www.batimes.com/articles/data-requirements-should-the-business-analyst-care.html

⇨ Data Flow Diagram Exercises with solutions
https://ssscsc2ab.wikispaces.com/file/view/DFD+Exercises+with+Solutions.pdf

⇨ Checking the Data Flow Diagrams for Errors
http://www.w3computing.com/systemsanalysis/checking-data-flow-diagrams-errors/

⇨ Capturing Data Requirements
http://www.slideshare.net/mcomtraining/capturing-data-requirements

⇨ Chapter 9 Describing Process Specifications and Structured Decisions (SOOADM)
https://sooadm.files.wordpress.com/2010/08/sooadm-chapter-9-describing-process-specifications-and-structured-decisions.pdf

THE BUSINESS VALUE OF DATA FLOW DIAGRAMS

Creating and Using DFD Fragments vs Completely Balanced DFDs

A completely balanced or levelled data flow diagram starts at the top with a context diagram consisting of one or more processes that are in scope for your project and all external entities with which those processes exchange data.

Each of those Level 1 processes explodes to a Level 2 data flow diagram depicting the detailed processes inside the Level 1 process with all internal data flows and data stores. Each process on the Level 2 diagram would either explode further to a Level 3 DFD (and from Level 3 to Level 4, etc.) or be described in detailed process specifications aka mini-specs.

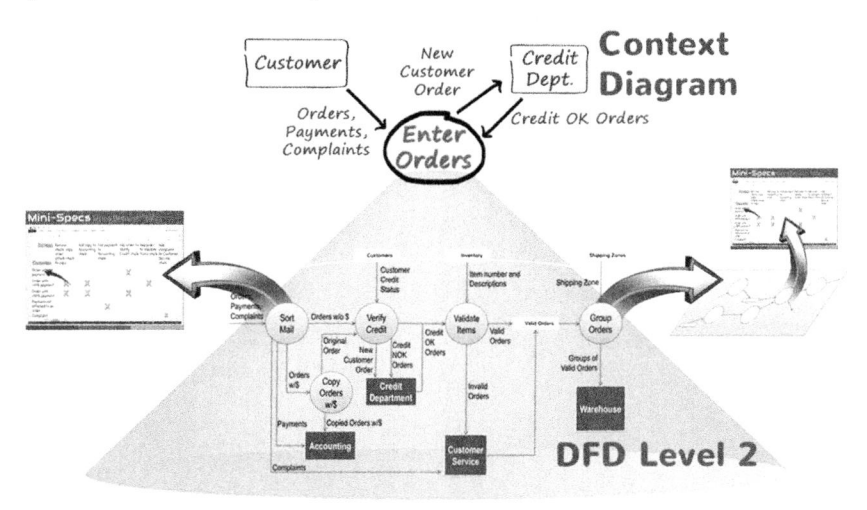

Processes that do not explode to a lower-level diagram are called 'Functional Primitives' and each data flow and each data store in the functional primitives should explode to a list of the contained data elements with their relevant metadata.

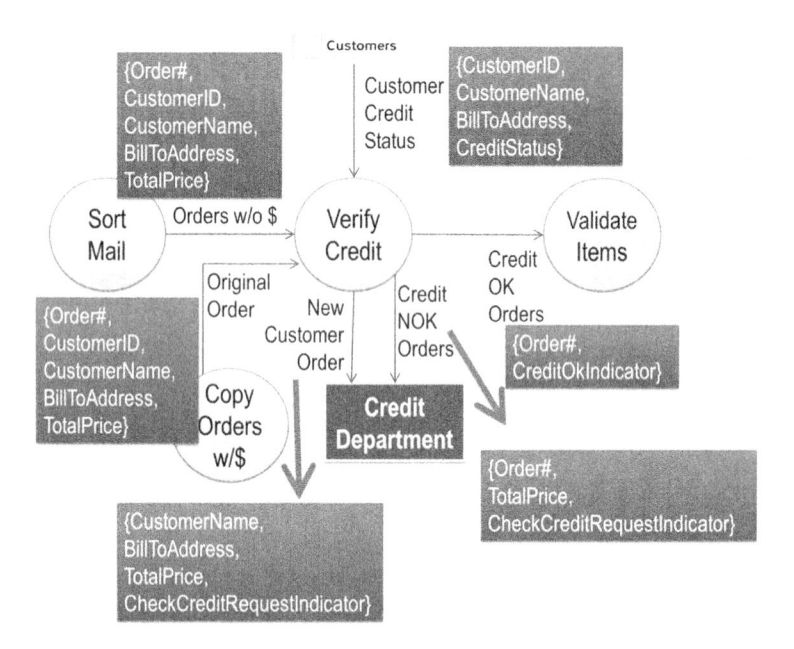

Although balancing a completely levelled DFD reveals data discrepancies and disconnects, it may not be necessary for your project. Many people only need a small fragment of a DFD to understand the inner workings of a specific process in particular on projects following an Agile approach to delivering technology.

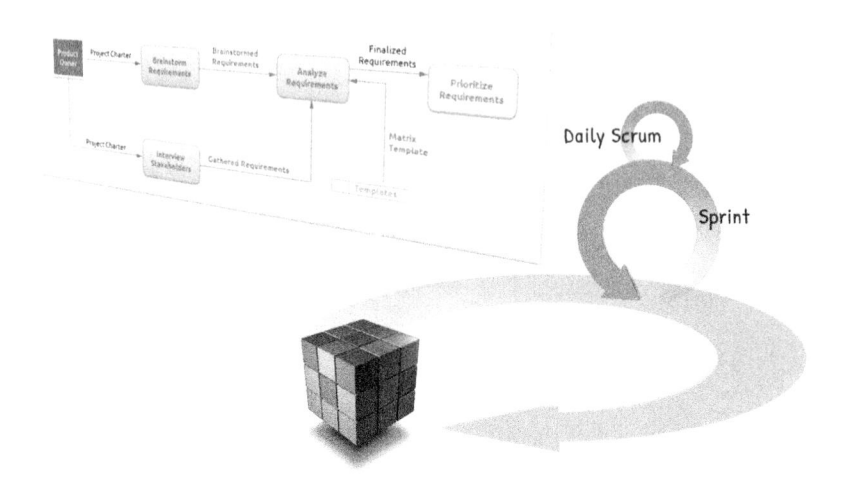

The time required to create a completely balanced diagram is not justified if a developer only needs to know how the CREDIT DEPARTMENT establishes the credit limit for a new customer. In that case, a DFD fragment might suffice.

The following is an example of a DFD fragment based on an exercise that we use in our instructor-led classes. To test your understanding of the concepts presented, you might want to take this opportunity to draw a DFD fragment using the project Scope Statement and the Interview Notes that follow before peeking at our solution.

Scope Statement:

This project will enhance our web-based Policy Maintenance System by allowing policyholders to interact directly with their insurance policies or claims. The system will support web-based policy payments and allow prospects to apply for temporary coverage pending underwriting rate approval. Once the application is received by Underwriting, it will follow standard Underwriting procedures.

Interview Notes:

In the future, a prospect will submit his/her application via our website. If the prospect does not yet have a policy with us, the site will request a credit check web service and either reject or approve the application directly. If the request is from one of our current customers in good standing or approved via the credit check, the site will provide a temporary proof of insurance certificate that the prospect can print out and use to register his/her vehicle. In any case, the request will then be forwarded to underwriting for normal processing, which will either lead to acceptance (the norm), modification (overriding a web rejection) or rejection (bad risk). If the request is approved, a policy will be issued and sent to the customer via standard mail.

Here is an example of the diagram that many of our students have produced for this scenario.

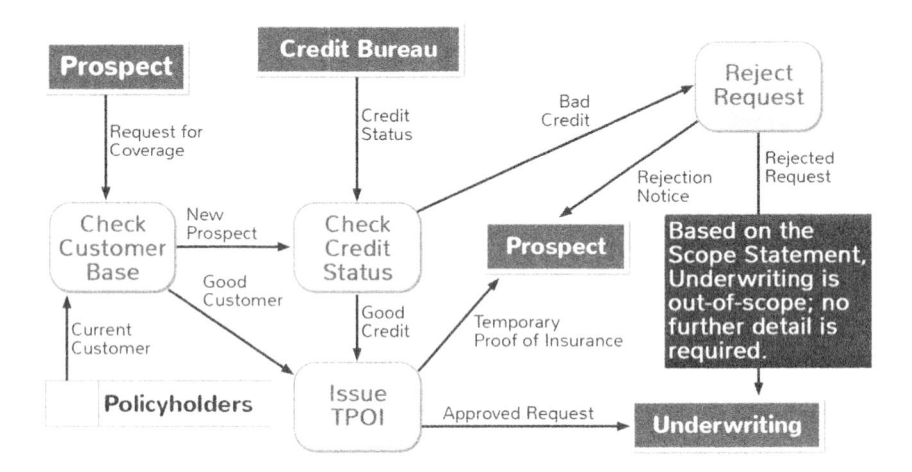

```
                          Credit Bureau
   Prospect                                          Reject
                                     Bad             Request
              Credit                 Credit
    Request   Status
    for                                              Rejected
    Coverage                         Rejection       Request
                                     Notice
    Check      New        Check                      Based on the
    Customer   Prospect   Credit      Prospect       Scope Statement,
    Base                  Status                     Underwriting is
               Good                                  out-of-scope; no
               Customer             Temporary        further detail is
    Current              Good       Proof of         required.
    Customer             Credit     Insurance

         Policyholders   Issue
                         TPOI       Approved Request Underwriting
```

Note that this DFD shows a business process at some *indeterminate level of detail*. Some of the processes might be very high-level whereas others are very specific. If you need to understand how any of these processes work in detail, you could "explode" it to see its internal processes.

Summary

From the perspective of the one wearing the BA hat, the act of creating a Data Flow Diagram (DFD) is an awakening. Drawing the diagram forces you to ask questions that you might otherwise overlook. It is also an awakening for members of the business community whose process you are depicting.

The people in the trenches and those managing them quite often have never seen a picture of their process and a picture activates parts of the human brain that words cannot. As a result, the phrase, "I see" takes on a whole different meaning when you are presented with a picture of your process.

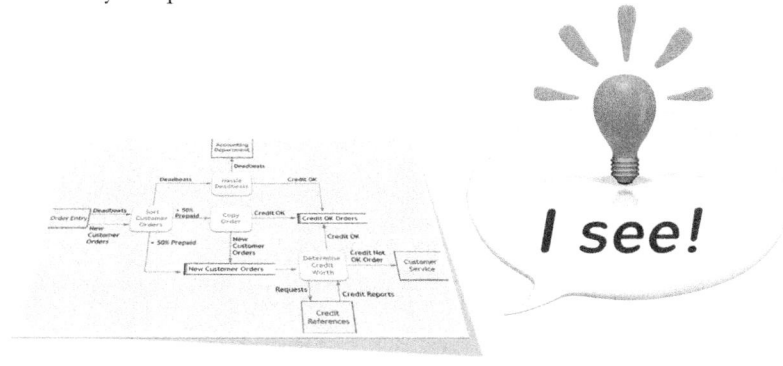

For that reason, I recommend drawing a DFD just to get everyone involved on the same page. Once you have a DFD, exploding a process and balancing the data inputs and outputs between the levels often reveals missed data flows. After all, no one can think of everything at once. If the tool finds a single missed data flow, it is probably well worth the time it took to draw the diagram and apply the technique.

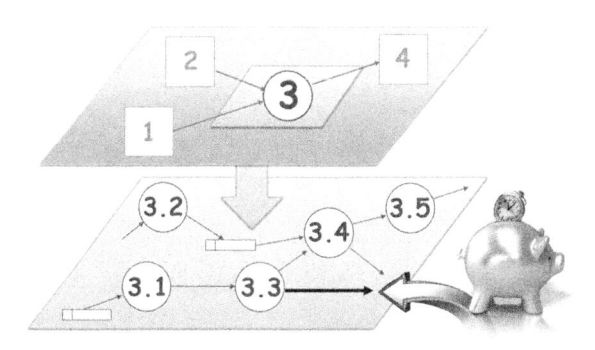

The same is true of horizontal balancing to reveal missing data elements. If we asked IT to automate a process with a missing data flow or data elements, we most likely will end up with an application that does not meet the business needs.

IT professionals are generally extremely good at their job and they will most likely recognize that they are missing something at some point in the development process. The problem is the timing of the discovery and the related cost when the omission is discovered. Adding a missing process late in the project is a relatively simple step, but missing data often affects a multitude of processes, making it one of the most expensive errors for IT projects.

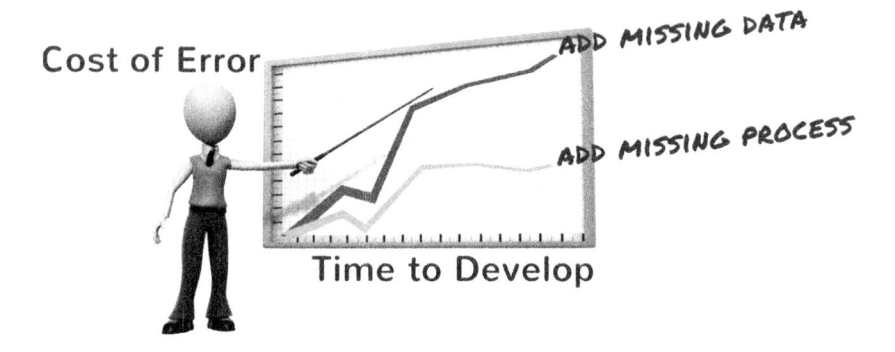

The simple act of identifying data elements and ensuring their completeness allows you to recognize and resolve these issues before you involve the developers. In my experience, that is one of the most powerful arguments for spending time to develop and analyze a data flow diagram.

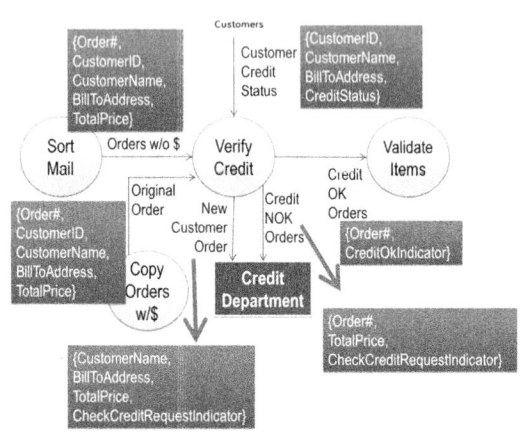

To summarize, creating a Data Flow Diagram is an extremely revealing and rewarding step in the analysis of a business process. I have never used any other tool that is as effective at triggering animated discussion amongst the stakeholders about how a business process works and how it should work.

Obviously, creating the diagram is just the first step. This diagram opens the door to a series of specific business analysis techniques that will help the business community recognize how their actions impact other downstream processes. You can also identify

- ☑ problem areas
- ☑ timing anomalies, and
- ☑ error handling issues

that can lead to missing requirements.

It is important to note that the diagram is a snapshot in time. Once you present the business community with this versatile visual aid, they may immediately start to make changes. Because of the cumulative effect of those changes, you should never assume that the diagram you created a few years or even a few months ago is valid. If you really need to understand the current business process, you are generally best served by starting from scratch as we demonstrated.

The problem you face is, of course, the effort required to flush out all of the details presented by levelling and balancing. Is it really worth the time? In our experience, a data flow diagram as a tool that benefits the project by reducing the risk of potential project failure can be worth its weight in gold. It is also amazing to experience how the diagram awakens project memories months or years later when you revisit it.

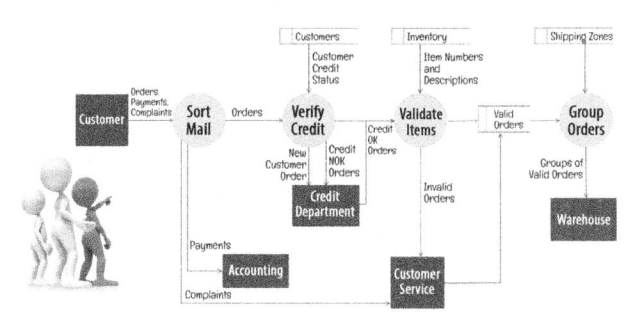

What Should You Do Next?

Thank you for reading, "Data Flow Diagrams – *Simply Put!*". We trust that you enjoyed the book, hope that you are able to integrate the presented ideas into your life, and that they serve you well when you are the one wearing the business analysis hat.

Any feedback you provide helps us improve the learning experience for all students. Please write a review on Amazon or our website ((http://goo.gl/O0HXaX) to capture your feedback. If you have any issues to report, we will respond as quickly as possible.

This book is just one component of our blended learning curriculum. Our discovery learning-based training approach and our other delivery methods (onsite/online classroom, self-paced eCourses, eBooks, and eMentoring) augment books such as this and allow you to select the appropriate combination to build your business analysis skills while containing costs. Check our Business Analysis Training Store (http://businessanalysisexperts.com/business-analysis-training-store/) for a complete overview of all of our training offers for the one wearing the BA hat.

Meanwhile, thank you again for buying this book. Use your new-found business analysis knowledge to achieve your personal and professional goals.

ABOUT THE AUTHORS

Angela and Tom Hathaway have authored and delivered hundreds of training courses and publications for business analysts around the world. They have facilitated hundreds of requirements discovery sessions for information technology projects under a variety of acronyms (JAD, ASAP, JADr, JRP, etc.). Based on their personal journey and experiences reported by their students, they recognized how much anyone can benefit from improving their requirements elicitation skills.

Angela's and Tom's mission is to allow anyone, anywhere access to simple, easy-to-learn business analysis techniques by sharing their experience and expertise in their business analysis training seminars, blogs, books, and public presentations.

At BA-EXPERTS (http://businessanalysisexperts.com/) we focus exclusively on Business Analysis for **"anyone wearing the BA hat™"**. We believe that business analysis has become a needed skill for every business professional whether or not they have the title Business Analyst. We have made it our goal to enable anyone wearing the BA hat™ to have access to high quality training material and performance support. Please call us at 702-637-4573, email us (Tom.Hathaway@ba-experts.com), or visit our Business Analyst Learning Store at (http://businessanalysisexperts.com/business-analysis-training-store/) if you are interested in other training offers. Amongst other offers, the content of this book is also available as an eCourse on our website.

Printed in Great Britain
by Amazon